OLD MOORE'S

HOROSCOPE AND ASTRAL DIARY

ARIES

OLD MOORE'S

HOROSCOPE AND ASTRAL DIARY

ARIES

foulsham

LONDON • NEW YORK • TORONTO • SYDNEY

foulsham

The Oriel, Thames Valley Court, 183–187 Bath Road, Slough,
Berkshire SL1 4AA, England

Foulsham books can be found in all good bookshops or direct from
www.foulsham.com

ISBN: 978-0-572-03504-4

A CIP record for this book is available from the British Library

Printed in Great Britain by CPI Cox & Wyman, Reading, RG1 8EX

CONTENTS

INTRODUCTION

Welcome to *Old Moore's Astral Diary* for the year 2010. The tradition of Old Moore and his astrological prowess goes right back to the 17th century and during that whole period Old Moore has been keeping track of Sun, Moon and planetary movement in order to provide humanity with the best knowledge of day-to-day astrology available.

These days humanity is slightly less fatalistic about the part the stars and planets play in our lives than it once was. Rather than seeing the zodiac as a harbinger of a good or bad fate, modern astrologers deal with the subtle interplay taking place above our heads. Astrology offers a better insight into the 'trends' that surround our lives at any particular time. When we are able to recognise how this or that solar, lunar or planetary position is likely to shape our days we can avoid certain actions or simply act at the right time to take advantage of what is on offer.

With the Astral Diary you can learn the best times to take advantage of positive monetary trends, choose when to pursue relationships and decide whether the time is right to make changes. Will you approach a day positively or with a little trepidation? This is the sort of question Old Moore can answer, and the Astral Diary gives you the chance to maximise your potential. When you see the sign ☿, this means that the planet Mercury is 'retrograde' at that time. Retrograde means that it appears to be moving backwards in space when viewed from Earth, and it indicates a little human disruption as a result. Mercury rules communication so you might expect a few setbacks in this area during this time. The Astral Diary also has space for you to add your own notes and comments.

Old Moore's Astral Diary is much more than a mere astrology book. It lets you look much deeper into your own individual nature. All that you are as an individual is reflected not only in the day but also in the time of day you were born. Your nature also responds to the position of heavenly bodies such as the Moon and the planet Venus. Using the unique tables in the Astral Diary you can work out exactly why you are the sort of person you turned out to be. Once in possession of this information you can deal much more effectively with the twists and turns of life and you will know better how to react to all trends.

Everything within your unique makeup is reflected within your astrological profile. Using the Astral Diary you can get close to the essence of planetary interplay, which in a moment-by-moment sense helps to shape your personality. Astrology can help you to maximise your potential and take those actions that lead to a happier life. Consulting *Old Moore's Astral Diary* will make you more aware of yourself, and is a fascinating way to register the very heartbeat of the solar system of which we are all a part.

Old Moore extends his customary greeting to all people of the Earth and offers his age-old wishes for a happy and prosperous period ahead.

THE ESSENCE
OF ARIES

Exploring the Personality of
Aries the Ram

(21ST MARCH – 20TH APRIL)

What's in a sign?

Aries is not the first sign of the zodiac by accident. It's the place in the year when the spring begins, and so it represents some of the most dynamic forces in nature, and within the zodiac as a whole. As a result the very essence of your nature is geared towards promoting yourself in life and pushing your ideas forward very positively. You don't brook a great deal of interference in your life, but you are quite willing to help others as much as you can, provided that to do so doesn't curb your natural desire to get on in life.

Aries people are not universally liked, though your true friends remain loyal to you under almost any circumstances. But why should it be that such a dynamic and go-getting person does meet with some opposition? The answer is simple: not everyone is quite so sure of themselves as you are and many tend to get nervous when faced with the sheer power of the Aries personality. If there is one factor within your own control that could counter these problems it is the adoption of some humility – that commodity which is so important for you to dredge from the depths of your nature. If you only show the world that you are human, and that you are well aware of the fact, most people would follow you willingly to the very gates of hell. The most successful Aries subjects know this fact and cultivate it to the full.

Your executive skills are never in doubt and you can get almost anything practical done whilst others are still jumping from foot to foot. That's why you are such a good organiser and are so likely to be out there at the front of any venture. Adventurous and quite willing to show your bravery in public, you can even surprise yourself sometimes with the limits you are likely to go to in order to reach solutions that seem right to you.

Kind to those you take to, you can be universally loved when working at your best. Despite this there will be times in your life when you simply can't understand why some people just don't like you. Maybe there's an element of jealousy involved.

Aries resources

The part of the zodiac occupied by the sign of Aries has, for many centuries, been recognised as the home of self-awareness. This means that there isn't a person anywhere else in the zodiac that has a better knowledge of self than you do. But this isn't necessarily an intellectual process with Aries, more a response to the very blood that is coursing through your veins. Aries' success doesn't so much come from spending hours working out the pros and cons of any given course of action, more from the thrill of actually getting stuck in. If you find yourself forced into a life that means constantly having to think everything through to the tiniest detail, there is likely to be some frustration in evidence.

Aries is ruled by Mars, arguably the most go-getting of all the planets in the solar system. Mars is martial and demands practical ways of expressing latent power. It also requires absolute obedience from subordinates. When this is forthcoming, Aries individuals are the most magnanimous people to be found anywhere. Loyalty is not a problem and there have been many instances in history when Aries people were quite willing to die for their friends if necessary.

When other people are willing to give up and go with the flow, you will still be out there pitching for the result that seems most advantageous to you. It isn't something you can particularly control and those who don't know you well could find you sometimes curt and over-demanding as a result. But because you are tenacious you can pick the bones out of any situation and will usually arrive at your desired destination, if you don't collapse with fatigue on the way.

Routines, or having to take life at the pace of less motivated types, won't suit you at all. Imprisonment of any sort, even in a failed relationship, is sheer torture and you will move heaven and earth to get out into the big, wide world, where you can exploit your natural potential to the full. Few people know you really well because you don't always explain yourself adequately. The ones who do adore you.

Beneath the surface

Whereas some zodiac signs are likely to spend a great deal of their lives looking carefully at the innermost recesses of their own minds, Aries individuals tend to prefer the cut and thrust of the practical world. Aries people are not natural philosophers, but that doesn't mean that you aren't just as complicated beneath the surface as any of your astrological brothers and sisters. So what is it that makes the Aries firebrand think and act in the way that it does? To a great extent it is a lack of basic self-confidence.

This statement might seem rather odd, bearing in mind that a fair percentage of the people running our world were born under the sign of the Ram, but it is true nevertheless. Why? Because people who know themselves and their capabilities really well don't feel the constant need to prove themselves in the way that is the driving force of your zodiac sign. Not that your naturally progressive tendencies are a fault. On the contrary, if used correctly they can help you to create a much better, fairer and happier world, at least in your own vicinity.

The fact that you occasionally take your ball and go home if you can't get your own way is really down to the same insecurity that is noticeable through many facets of your nature. If Aries can't rule, it often doesn't want to play at all. A deep resentment and a brooding quality can build up in the minds and souls of some thwarted Aries types, a tendency that you need to combat. Better by far to try and compromise, itself a word that doesn't exist in the vocabularies of the least enlightened people born under the sign of the Ram. Once this lesson is learned, inner happiness increases and you relax into your life much more.

The way you think about others is directly related to the way you consider they think about you. This leads to another surprising fact regarding the zodiac sign. Aries people absolutely hate to be disliked, though they would move heaven and earth to prove that this isn't the case. And as a result Aries both loves and hates with a passion. Deep inside you can sometimes be a child shivering in the dark. If you only realise this fact your path to happiness and success is almost assured. Of course to do so takes a good deal of courage – but that's a commodity you don't lack.

Making the best of yourself

It would be quite clear to any observer that you are not the sort of person who likes to hang around at the back of a queue, or who would relish constantly taking orders from people who may not know situations as well as you do. For that reason alone you are better in positions that see you out there at the front, giving commands and enjoying the cut and thrust of everyday life. In a career sense this means that whatever you do you are happiest telling those around you how to do it too. Many Aries people quite naturally find their way to the top of the tree and don't usually have too much trouble staying there.

It is important to remember, however, that there is another side to your nature: the giving qualities beneath your natural dominance. You can always be around when people need you the most, encouraging and even gently pushing when it is necessary. By keeping friends and being willing to nurture relationships across a broad spectrum, you gradually get to know what makes those around you tick. This makes for a more patient and understanding sort of Aries subject – the most potent of all.

Even your resilience is not endless, which is why it is important to remember that there are times when you need rest. Bearing in mind that you are not superhuman is the hardest lesson to learn, but the admission brings humility, something that Aries needs to cultivate whenever possible.

Try to avoid living a restricted life and make your social contacts frequent and important. Realise that there is much more to life than work and spend some of your free time genuinely attempting to help those who are less well off than you are. Crucially you must remember that 'help' is not the same as domination.

The impressions you give

This section may well be of less interest to Aries subjects than it would be to certain other zodiac signs. The reason is quite clear. Aries people are far less interested in what others think about them than almost anyone else – or at least they tell themselves that they are. Either way it is counterproductive to ignore the opinions of the world at large because to do so creates stumbling blocks, even in a practical sense.

Those around you probably find you extremely capable and well able to deal with almost any situation that comes your way. Most are willing to rely heavily on you and the majority would almost instinctively see you as a leader. Whether or not they like you at the same time is really dependent on the way you handle situations. That's the difference between the go-getting, sometimes selfish type of Aries subject and the more enlightened amongst this illustrious sign.

You are viewed as being exciting and well able to raise enthusiasm for almost any project that takes your fancy. Of course this implies a great responsibility because you are always expected to come up with the goods. The world tends to put certain people on a pedestal, and you are one of them. On the other side of the coin we are all inclined to fire arrows at the elevated, so maintaining your position isn't very easy.

Most of the time you are seen as being magnanimous and kind, factors that you can exploit, whilst at the same time recognising the depth of the responsibility that comes with being an Aries subject. It might not be a bad thing to allow those around you to see that you too have feet of clay. This will make them respect and support you all the more, and even Aries people really do need to feel loved. A well-balanced Aries subject is one of the most elevated spirits to be found anywhere.

The way forward

You certainly enjoy life more when looking at it from the top of the tree. Struggling to get by is not in the least interesting to your zodiac sign and you can soon become miserable if things are not going well for you. That's why it is probably quite justified in your case to work tenaciously in order to achieve your objectives. Ideally, once you have realised some sort of success and security for yourself, you should then be willing to sit and watch life go by a little more. In fact this doesn't happen. The reason for this is clear. The Aries subject who learns how to succeed rarely knows when to stop – it's as simple as that.

Splitting your life into different components can help, if only because this means that you don't get the various elements mixed up. So, for example, don't confuse your love life with your professional needs, or your family with colleagues. This process allows you to view life in manageable chunks and also makes it possible for you to realise when any one of them may be working well. As a result you will put the effort where it's needed, and enjoy what is going well for you.

If you want to know real happiness you will also have to learn that acquisition for its own sake brings hollow rewards at best. When your talents are being turned outward to the world at large, you are one of the most potent and successful people around. What is more you should find yourself to be a much happier person when you are lending a hand to the wider world. This is possible, maybe outside of your normal professional sphere, though even where voluntary work is concerned it is important not to push yourself to the point of fatigue.

Keep yourself physically fit, without necessarily expecting that you can run to the South Pole and back, and stay away from too many stimulants, such as alcohol and nicotine. The fact is that you are best when living a healthy life, but it doesn't help either if you make even abstinence into an art form. Balance is important, as is moderation – itself a word that is difficult for you to understand. In terms of your approach to other people it's important to realise that everyone has a specific point of view. These might be different to yours, but they are not necessarily wrong. Sort out the friends who are most important to you and stick with them, whilst at the same time realising that almost everyone can be a pal – with just a little effort.

ARIES ON THE CUSP

Old Moore is often asked how astrological profiles are altered for those people born at either the beginning or the end of a zodiac sign, or, more properly, on the cusps of a sign. In the case of Aries this would be on the 21st of March and for two or three days after, and similarly at the end of the sign, probably from the 18th to the 20th of April. In this year's Astral Diaries, once again, Old Moore sets out to explain the differences regarding cuspid signs.

The Pisces Cusp – March 21st to March 24th

With the Sun so close to the zodiac sign of Pisces at the time you were born, it is distinctly possible that you have always had some doubts when reading a character breakdown written specifically for the sign of Aries. This isn't surprising because no zodiac sign has a definite start or end, they merely merge together. As a result there are some of the characteristics of the sign of the Fishes that are intermingled with the qualities of Aries in your nature.

What we probably find, as a result, is a greater degree of emotional sensitivity and a tendency to be more cognisant of what the rest of humanity is feeling. This is not to imply that Aries is unfeeling, but rather that Pisceans actively make humanity their business.

You are still able to achieve your most desired objectives in the practical world, but on the way, you stop to listen to the heartbeat of the planet on which you live. A very good thing, of course, but at the same time there is some conflict created if your slightly dream-like tendencies get in the way of your absolute need to see things through to their logical conclusion.

Nobody knows you better than you know yourself, or at least that's what the Aries qualities within you say, but that isn't always verified by some of the self-doubt that comes from the direction of the Fishes. As in all matters astrological, a position of balance has to be achieved in order to reconcile the differing qualities of your nature. In your case, this is best accomplished by being willing to stop and think once in a while and by refusing to allow your depth to be a problem.

Dealt with properly, the conjoining of Pisces and Aries can be a wondrous and joyful affair, a harmony of opposites that always makes you interesting to know. Your position in the world is naturally one of authority but at the same time you need to serve. That's why some people with this sort of mixture of astrological qualities would make such good administrators in a hospital, or in any position where the alternate astrological needs are well balanced. In the chocolate box of life you are certainly a 'soft centre'.

The Taurus Cusp – April 18th to April 20th

The merge from Aries to Taurus is much less well defined than the one at the other side of Aries, but it can be very useful to you all the same. Like the Pisces-influenced Aries you may be slightly more quiet than would be the case with the Ram taken alone and your thought processes are probably not quite as fast. But to compensate for this fact you don't rush into things quite as much and are willing to allow ideas to mature more fully.

Your sense of harmony and beauty is strong and you know, in a very definite way, exactly what you want. As a result your home will be distinctive but tasteful and it's a place where you need space to be alone sometimes, which the true Aries subject probably does not. You do not lack the confidence to make things look the way you want them, but you have a need to display these things to the world at large and sometimes even to talk about how good you are at decoration and design.

If anyone finds you pushy, it is probably because they don't really know what makes you tick. Although you are willing to mix with almost anyone, you are more inclined, at base, to have a few very close friends who stay at the forefront of your life for a long time. It is likely that you enjoy refined company and you wouldn't take kindly to the dark, the sordid, or the downright crude in life.

Things don't get you down as much as can sometimes be seen to be the case for Taurus when taken alone and you are rarely stumped for a progressive and practical idea when one is needed most. At all levels, your creative energy is evident and some of you even have the ability to make this into a business, since Aries offers the practical and administrative spark that Taurus can sometimes lack.

In matters of love, you are ardent and sincere, probably an idealist, and you know what you want in a partner. Whilst this is also true in the case of Taurus, you are different, because you are much more likely, not only to look, but also to say something about the way you feel.

Being naturally friendly you rarely go short of the right sort of help and support when it is most vital. Part of the reason for this lies in the fact that you are so willing to be the sounding-board for the concerns of your friends. All in all you can be very contented with your lot, but you never stop searching for something better all the same. At its best, this is one of the most progressive cuspal matches of them all.

ARIES AND ITS ASCENDANTS

The nature of every individual on the planet is composed of the rich variety of zodiac signs and planetary positions that were present at the time of their birth. Your Sun sign, which in your case is Aries, is one of the many factors when it comes to assessing the unique person you are. Probably the most important consideration, other than your Sun sign, is to establish the zodiac sign that was rising over the eastern horizon at the time that you were born. This is your Ascending or Rising sign. Most popular astrology fails to take account of the Ascendant, and yet its importance remains with you from the very moment of your birth, through every day of your life. The Ascendant is evident in the way you approach the world, and so, when meeting a person for the first time, it is this astrological influence that you are most likely to notice first. Our Ascending sign essentially represents what we appear to be, while our Sun sign is what we feel inside ourselves.

The Ascendant also has the potential for modifying our overall nature. For example, if you were born at a time of day when Aries was passing over the eastern horizon (this would be around the time of dawn) then you would be classed as a double Aries. As such you would typify this zodiac sign, both internally and in your dealings with others. However, if your Ascendant sign turned out to be a Water sign, such as Pisces, there would be a profound alteration of nature, away from the expected qualities of Aries.

One of the reasons that popular astrology often ignores the Ascendant is that it has always been rather difficult to establish. Old Moore has found a way to make this possible by devising an easy-to-use table, which you will find on page 158 of this book. Using this, you can establish your Ascendant sign at a glance. You will need to know your rough time of birth, then it is simply a case of following the instructions.

For those readers who have no idea of their time of birth it might be worth allowing a good friend, or perhaps your partner, to read through the section that follows this introduction. Someone who deals with you on a regular basis may easily discover your Ascending sign, even though you could have some difficulty establishing it for yourself. A good understanding of this component of your nature is essential if you want to be aware of that 'other person' who is responsible for the way you make contact with the world at large. Your Sun sign, Ascendant sign, and the other pointers in this book will, together, allow you a far better understanding of what makes you tick as an individual. Peeling back the different layers of your astrological make-up can be an enlightening experience, and the Ascendant may represent one of the most important layers of all.

Aries with Aries Ascendant

What you see is what you get with this combination. You typify the no-nonsense approach of Aries at its best. All the same this combination is quite daunting when viewed through the eyes of other, less dominant sorts of people. You tend to push your way though situations that would find others cowering in a corner and you are afraid of very little. With a determination to succeed that makes you a force to be reckoned with, you leave the world in no doubt as to your intentions and tend to be rather too brusque for your own good on occasions.

At heart you are kind and loving, able to offer assistance to the downtrodden and sad, and usually willing to take on board the cares of people who have a part to play in your life. No-one would doubt your sincerity, or your honesty, though you may utilise slightly less than orthodox ways of getting your own way on those occasions when you feel you have right on your side. You are a loving partner and a good parent, though where children are concerned you tend to be rather too protective. The trouble is that you know what a big, bad world it can be and probably feel that you are better equipped to deal with things than anyone else.

Aries with Taurus Ascendant

This is a much quieter combination, so much so that even experienced astrologers would be unlikely to recognise you as an Aries subject at all, unless of course they came to know you very well. Your approach to life tends to be quiet and considered and there is a great danger that you could suppress those feelings that others of your kind would be only too willing to verbalise. To compensate you are deeply creative and will think matters through much more readily than more dominant Aries types would be inclined to do. Reaching out towards the world, you are, nevertheless, somewhat locked inside yourself and can struggle to achieve the level of communication that you so desperately need. Frustration might easily follow, were it not for the fact that you possess a quiet determination that, to those in the know, is the clearest window through to your Aries soul.

The care for others is stronger here than with almost any other Aries type and you certainly demonstrate this at all levels. The fact is that you live a great percentage of your life in service to the people you take to, whilst at the same time being able to shut the door firmly in the face of people who irritate or anger you. You are deeply motivated towards family relationships.

Aries with Gemini Ascendant

A fairly jolly combination this, though by no means easy for others to come to terms with. You fly about from pillar to post and rarely stop long enough to take a breath. Admittedly this suits your own needs very well, but it can be a source of some disquiet to those around you, since they may not possess your energy or motivation. Those who know you well are deeply in awe of your capacity to keep going long after almost everyone else would have given up and gone home, though this quality is not always as wonderful as it sounds because it means that you put more pressure on your nervous system than just about any other astrological combination.

You need to be mindful of your nervous system, which responds to the erratic, mercurial quality of Gemini. Problems only really arise when the Aries part of you makes demands that the Gemini component finds difficult to deal with. There are paradoxes galore here and some of them need sorting out if you are ever fully to understand yourself, or are to be in a position when others know what makes you tick.

In relationships you might be a little fickle, but you are a real charmer and never stuck for the right words, no matter who you are dealing with. Your tenacity knows no bounds, though perhaps it should!

Aries with Cancer Ascendant

The main problem that you experience in life shows itself as a direct result of the meshing of these two very different zodiac signs. At heart Aries needs to dominate, whereas Cancer shows a desire to nurture. All too often the result can be a protective arm that is so strong that nobody could possibly get out from under it. Lighten your own load, and that of those you care for, by being willing to sit back and watch others please themselves a little. You might think that you know best, and your heart is clearly in the right place, but try to realise what life is like when someone is always on hand to tell you that they know better then you do.

But in a way this is a little severe, because you are fairly intuitive and your instincts would rarely lead you astray. Nobody could ask for a better partner or parent than you, though they might request a slightly less attentive one. In matters of work you are conscientious and are probably best suited to a job that means sorting out the kind of mess that humanity is so good at creating. You probably spend your spare time untangling balls of wool, though you are quite sporting too and could easily make the Olympics. Once there you would not win however, because you would be too concerned about all the other competitors.

Aries with Leo Ascendant

Here we come upon the first situation of Aries being allied with another Fire sign. This creates a character that could appear to be typically Aries at first sight and in many ways it is, though there are subtle differences that should not be ignored. Although you have the typical Aries ability to get things done, many of the tasks you do undertake will be for and on behalf of others. You can be proud, and on some occasions even haughty, and yet you are also regal in your bearing and honest to the point of absurdity. Nobody could doubt your sincerity and you have the soul of a poet combined with the courage of a lion.

All this is good, but it makes you rather difficult to approach, unless the person in question has first adopted a crouching and subservient attitude although you would not wish them to do so. It's simply that the impression you give and the motivation that underpins it are two quite different things. You are greatly respected and in the case of those individuals who know your real nature, you are also deeply loved. But life would be much simpler if you didn't always have to fight the wars that those around you are happy to start. Relaxation is a word that you don't really understand and you would do yourself a favour if you looked it up in a dictionary.

Aries with Virgo Ascendant

Virgo is steady and sure, though also fussy and stubborn. Aries is fast and determined, restless and active. It can already be seen that this is a rather strange meeting of characteristics and because Virgo is ruled by the capricious Mercury, the ultimate result will change from hour to hour and day to day. It isn't merely that others find it difficult to know where they are with you, they can't even understand what makes you tick. This will make you the subject of endless fascination and attention, at which you will be apparently surprised but inwardly pleased. If anyone ever really gets to know what goes on in that busy mind they may find the implications very difficult to deal with and it is a fact that only you would have the ability to live inside your crowded head.

As a partner and a parent you are second to none, though you tend to get on better with your children once they start to grow, since by this time you may be slightly less restricting to their own desires, which will often clash with your own on their behalf. You are capable of give and take and could certainly not be considered selfish, though your constant desire to get the best from everyone might occasionally be misconstrued.

Aries with Libra Ascendant

Libra has the tendency to bring out the best in any zodiac sign, and this is no exception when it comes together with Aries. You may, in fact, be the most comfortable of all Aries types, simply because Libra tempers some of your more assertive qualities and gives you the chance to balance out opposing forces, both inside yourself and in the world outside. You are fun to be with and make the staunchest friend possible. Although you are generally affable, few people would try to put one over on you, because they would quickly come to know how far you are willing to go before you let forth a string of invective that would shock those who previously underestimated your basic Aries traits.

Home and family are very dear to you, but you are more tolerant than some Aries types are inclined to be and you have a youthful zest for life that should stay with you no matter what age you manage to achieve. There is always something interesting to do and your mind is a constant stream of possibilities. This makes you very creative and you may also demonstrate a desire to look good at all times. You may not always be quite as confident as you appear to be, but few would guess the fact.

Aries with Scorpio Ascendant

The two very different faces of Mars come together in this potent, magnetic and quite awe-inspiring combination. Your natural inclination is towards secrecy and this fact, together with the natural attractions of the sensual Scorpio nature, makes you the object of great curiosity. This means that you will not go short of attention and should ensure that you are always being analysed by people who may never get to know you at all. At heart you prefer your own company, and yet life appears to find means to push you into the public gaze time and again. Most people with this combination ooze sex appeal and can use this fact as a stepping stone to personal success, yet without losing any integrity or loosening the cords of a deeply moralistic nature.

On those occasions when you do lose your temper, there isn't a character in the length and breadth of the zodiac who would have either the words or the courage to stand against the stream of invective that follows. On really rare occasions you might even scare yourself. As far as family members are concerned a simple look should be enough to show when you are not amused. Few people are left unmoved by your presence in their life.

Aries with Sagittarius Ascendant

What a lovely combination this can be, for the devil-may-care aspects of Sagittarius lighten the load of a sometimes too-serious Aries interior. Everything that glistens is not gold, though it's hard to convince you of the fact because, to mix metaphors, you can make a silk purse out of a sow's ear. Almost everyone loves you and in return you offer a friendship that is warm and protective, but not as demanding as sometimes tends to be the case with the Aries type. Relationships may be many and varied and there is often more than one major attachment in the life of those holding this combination. You will bring a breath of spring to any attachment, though you need to ensure that the person concerned is capable of keeping up with the hectic pace of your life.

It may appear from time to time that you are rather too trusting for your own good, though deep inside you are very astute and it seems that almost everything you undertake works out well in the end. This has nothing to do with native luck and is really down to the fact that you are much more calculating than might appear to be the case at first sight. As a parent you are protective yet offer sufficient room for self-expression.

Aries with Capricorn Ascendant

If ever anyone could be accused of setting off immediately, but slowly, it has to be you. These are very contradictory signs and the differences will express themselves in a variety of ways. One thing is certain, you have tremendous tenacity and will see a job through patiently from beginning to end, without tiring on the way, and ensuring that every detail is taken care of properly. This combination often bestows good health and a great capacity for continuity, particularly in terms of the length of life. You are certainly not as argumentative as the typical Aries, but you do know how to get your own way, which is just as well because you are usually thinking on behalf of everyone else and not just on your own account.

At home you can relax, which is a blessing for Aries, though in fact you seldom choose to do so because you always have some project or other on the go. You probably enjoy knocking down and rebuilding walls, though this is a practical tendency and not responsive to relationships, in which you are ardent and sincere. Impetuosity is as close to your heart as is the case for any type of Aries subject, though you certainly have the ability to appear patient and steady. But it's just a front, isn't it?

Aries with Aquarius Ascendant

The person standing on a soap box in the corner of the park, extolling the virtues of this or that, could quite easily be an Aries with an Aquarian Ascendant. You are certainly not averse to speaking your mind and you have plenty to talk about because you are the best social reformer and political animal of them all. Unorthodox in your approach, you have the ability to keep everyone guessing, except when it comes to getting your own way, for in this nobody doubts your natural abilities. You can put theories into practice very well and on the way you retain a sense of individuality that would shock more conservative types. It's true that a few people might find you a little difficult to approach and this is partly because you have an inner reserve and strength which is difficult for others to fathom.

In the world at large you take your place at the front, as any good Arian should, and yet you offer room for others to share your platform. You keep up with the latest innovations and treat family members as the genuine friends that you believe them to be. Care needs to be taken when picking a life partner, for you are an original, and not just anyone could match the peculiarities thrown up by this astrological combination.

Aries with Pisces Ascendant

Although not an easy combination to deal with, the Aries with a Piscean Ascendant does, nevertheless, bring something very special to the world in the way of natural understanding allied to practical assistance. It's true that you can sometimes be a dreamer, but there is nothing wrong with that as long as you have the ability to turn some of your wishes into reality, and this you are easily able to do, usually for the sake of those around you. Conversation comes easily to you, though you also possess a slightly wistful and poetic side to your nature, which is attractive to the many people who call you a friend. A natural entertainer, you bring a sense of the comic to the often serious qualities of Aries, though without losing the determination that typifies the sign.

In relationships you are ardent, sincere and supportive, with a strong social conscience that sometimes finds you fighting the battles of the less privileged members of society. Family is important to you and this is a combination that invariably leads to parenthood. Away from the cut and thrust of everyday life you relax more fully and think about matters more deeply than more typical Aries types might.

THE MOON AND THE PART IT PLAYS IN YOUR LIFE

In astrology the Moon is probably the single most important heavenly body after the Sun. Its unique position, as partner to the Earth on its journey around the solar system, means that the Moon appears to pass through the signs of the zodiac extremely quickly. The zodiac position of the Moon at the time of your birth plays a great part in personal character and is especially significant in the build-up of your emotional nature.

Sun Moon Cycles

The first lunar cycle deals with the part the position of the Moon plays relative to your Sun sign. I have made the fluctuations of this pattern easy for you to understand by means of a simple cyclic graph. It appears on the first page of each 'Your Month At A Glance', under the title 'Highs and Lows'. The graph displays the lunar cycle and you will soon learn to understand how its movements have a bearing on your level of energy and your abilities.

Your Own Moon Sign

Discovering the position of the Moon at the time of your birth has always been notoriously difficult because tracking the complex zodiac positions of the Moon is not easy. This process has been reduced to three simple stages with Old Moore's unique Lunar Tables. A breakdown of the Moon's zodiac positions can be found from page 25 onwards, so that once you know what your Moon Sign is, you can see what part this plays in the overall build-up of your personal character.

If you follow the instructions on the next page you will soon be able to work out exactly what zodiac sign the Moon occupied on the day that you were born and you can then go on to compare the reading for this position with those of your Sun sign and your Ascendant. It is partly the comparison between these three important positions that goes towards making you the unique individual you are.

HOW TO DISCOVER YOUR MOON SIGN

This is a three-stage process. You may need a pen and a piece of paper but if you follow the instructions below the process should only take a minute or so.

STAGE 1 First of all you need to know the Moon Age at the time of your birth. If you look at Moon Table 1, on page 23, you will find all the years between 1912 and 2010 down the left side. Find the year of your birth and then trace across to the right to the month of your birth. Where the two intersect you will find a number. This is the date of the New Moon in the month that you were born. You now need to count forward the number of days between the New Moon and your own birthday. For example, if the New Moon in the month of your birth was shown as being the 6th and you were born on the 20th, your Moon Age Day would be 14. If the New Moon in the month of your birth came after your birthday, you need to count forward from the New Moon in the previous month. If you were born in a Leap Year, remember to count the 29th February. You can tell if your birth year was a Leap Year if the last two digits can be divided by four. Whatever the result, jot this number down so that you do not forget it.

STAGE 2 Take a look at Moon Table 2 on page 24. Down the left hand column look for the date of your birth. Now trace across to the month of your birth. Where the two meet you will find a letter. Copy this letter down alongside your Moon Age Day.

STAGE 3 Moon Table 3 on page 24 will supply you with the zodiac sign the Moon occupied on the day of your birth. Look for your Moon Age Day down the left hand column and then for the letter you found in Stage 2. Where the two converge you will find a zodiac sign and this is the sign occupied by the Moon on the day that you were born.

Your Zodiac Moon Sign Explained

You will find a profile of all zodiac Moon Signs on pages 25 to 28, showing in yet another way how astrology helps to make you into the individual that you are. In each daily entry of the Astral Diary you can find the zodiac position of the Moon for every day of the year. This also allows you to discover your lunar birthdays. Since the Moon passes through all the signs of the zodiac in about a month, you can expect something like twelve lunar birthdays each year. At these times you are likely to be emotionally steady and able to make the sort of decisions that have real, lasting value.

MOON TABLE 1

YEAR	FEB	MAR	APR	YEAR	FEB	MAR	APR	YEAR	FEB	MAR	APR
1912	17	19	18	1945	12	14	12	1978	7	9	7
1913	6	7	6	1946	2	3	2	1979	26	27	26
1914	24	26	24	1947	19	21	20	1980	15	16	15
1915	14	15	13	1948	9	11	9	1981	4	6	4
1916	3	5	3	1949	27	29	28	1982	23	24	23
1917	22	23	22	1950	16	18	17	1983	13	14	13
1918	11	12	11	1951	6	7	6	1984	1	2	1
1919	–	2/31	30	1952	25	25	24	1985	19	21	20
1920	19	20	18	1953	14	15	13	1986	9	10	9
1921	8	9	8	1954	3	5	3	1987	28	29	28
1922	26	28	27	1955	22	24	22	1988	17	18	16
1923	15	17	16	1956	11	12	11	1989	6	7	6
1924	5	5	4	1957	–	1/31	29	1990	25	26	25
1925	23	24	23	1958	18	20	19	1991	14	15	13
1926	12	14	12	1959	7	9	8	1992	3	4	3
1927	2	3	2	1960	26	27	26	1993	22	24	22
1928	19	21	20	1961	15	16	15	1994	10	12	11
1929	9	11	9	1962	5	6	5	1995	29	30	29
1930	28	30	28	1963	23	25	23	1996	18	19	18
1931	17	19	18	1964	13	14	12	1997	7	9	7
1932	6	7	6	1965	1	2	1	1998	26	27	26
1933	24	26	24	1966	19	21	20	1999	16	17	16
1934	14	15	13	1967	9	10	9	2000	5	6	4
1935	3	5	3	1968	28	29	28	2001	23	24	23
1936	22	23	21	1969	17	18	16	2002	12	13	12
1937	11	13	12	1970	6	7	6	2003	–	2	1
1938	–	2/31	30	1971	25	26	25	2004	20	21	19
1939	19	20	19	1972	14	15	13	2005	9	10	8
1940	8	9	7	1973	4	5	3	2006	28	29	27
1941	26	27	26	1974	22	24	22	2007	16	18	17
1942	15	16	15	1975	11	12	11	2008	6	7	6
1943	4	6	4	1976	29	30	29	2009	25	26	25
1944	24	24	22	1977	18	19	18	2010	14	15	14

TABLE 2

DAY	MAR	APR
1	F	J
2	G	J
3	G	J
4	G	J
5	G	J
6	G	J
7	G	J
8	G	J
9	G	J
10	G	J
11	G	K
12	H	K
13	H	K
14	H	K
15	H	K
16	H	K
17	H	K
18	H	K
19	H	K
20	H	K
21	H	L
22	I	L
23	I	L
24	I	L
25	I	L
26	I	L
27	I	L
28	I	L
29	I	L
30	I	L
31	I	–

MOON TABLE 3

M/D	F	G	H	I	J	K	L
0	PI	PI	AR	AR	AR	TA	TA
1	PI	AR	AR	AR	TA	TA	TA
2	AR	AR	AR	TA	TA	TA	GE
3	AR	AR	TA	TA	TA	GE	GE
4	AR	TA	TA	GE	GE	GE	GE
5	TA	TA	GE	GE	GE	CA	CA
6	TA	GE	GE	GE	CA	CA	CA
7	GE	GE	GE	CA	CA	CA	LE
8	GE	GE	CA	CA	CA	LE	LE
9	CA	CA	CA	CA	LE	LE	VI
10	CA	CA	LE	LE	LE	VI	VI
11	CA	LE	LE	LE	VI	VI	VI
12	LE	LE	LE	VI	VI	VI	LI
13	LE	LE	VI	VI	VI	LI	LI
14	VI	VI	VI	LI	LI	LI	LI
15	VI	VI	LI	LI	LI	SC	SC
16	VI	LI	LI	LI	SC	SC	SC
17	LI	LI	LI	SC	SC	SC	SA
18	LI	LI	SC	SC	SC	SA	SA
19	LI	SC	SC	SC	SA	SA	SA
20	SC	SC	SA	SA	SA	CP	CP
21	SC	SA	SA	SA	CP	CP	CP
22	SC	SA	SA	CP	CP	CP	AQ
23	SA	SA	CP	CP	CP	AQ	AQ
24	SA	CP	CP	CP	AQ	AQ	AQ
25	CP	CP	AQ	AQ	AQ	PI	PI
26	CP	AQ	AQ	AQ	PI	PI	PI
27	AQ	AQ	AQ	PI	PI	PI	AR
28	AQ	AQ	PI	PI	PI	AR	AR
29	AQ	PI	PI	PI	AR	AR	AR

AR = Aries, TA = Taurus, GE = Gemini, CA = Cancer, LE = Leo, VI = Virgo, LI = Libra, SC = Scorpio, SA = Sagittarius, CP = Capricorn, AQ = Aquarius, PI = Pisces

MOON SIGNS

Moon in Aries

You have a strong imagination, courage, determination and a desire to do things in your own way and forge your own path through life.

Originality is a key attribute; you are seldom stuck for ideas although your mind is changeable and you could take the time to focus on individual tasks. Often quick-tempered, you take orders from few people and live life at a fast pace. Avoid health problems by taking regular time out for rest and relaxation.

Emotionally, it is important that you talk to those you are closest to and work out your true feelings. Once you discover that people are there to help, there is less necessity for you to do everything yourself.

Moon in Taurus

The Moon in Taurus gives you a courteous and friendly manner, which means you are likely to have many friends.

The good things in life mean a lot to you, as Taurus is an Earth sign that delights in experiences which please the senses. Hence you are probably a lover of good food and drink, which may in turn mean you need to keep an eye on the bathroom scales, especially as looking good is also important to you.

Emotionally you are fairly stable and you stick by your own standards. Taureans do not respond well to change. Intuition also plays an important part in your life.

Moon in Gemini

You have a warm-hearted character, sympathetic and eager to help others. At times reserved, you can also be articulate and chatty: this is part of the paradox of Gemini, which always brings duplicity to the nature. You are interested in current affairs, have a good intellect, and are good company and likely to have many friends. Most of your friends have a high opinion of you and would be ready to defend you should the need arise. However, this is usually unnecessary, as you are quite capable of defending yourself in any verbal confrontation.

Travel is important to your inquisitive mind and you find intellectual stimulus in mixing with people from different cultures. You also gain much from reading, writing and the arts but you do need plenty of rest and relaxation in order to avoid fatigue.

Moon in Cancer

The Moon in Cancer at the time of birth is a fortunate position as Cancer is the Moon's natural home. This means that the qualities of compassion and understanding given by the Moon are especially enhanced in your nature, and you are friendly and sociable and cope well with emotional pressures. You cherish home and family life, and happily do the domestic tasks. Your surroundings are important to you and you hate squalor and filth. You are likely to have a love of music and poetry.

Your basic character, although at times changeable like the Moon itself, depends on symmetry. You aim to make your surroundings comfortable and harmonious, for yourself and those close to you.

Moon in Leo

The best qualities of the Moon and Leo come together to make you warm-hearted, fair, ambitious and self-confident. With good organisational abilities, you invariably rise to a position of responsibility in your chosen career. This is fortunate as you don't enjoy being an 'also-ran' and would rather be an important part of a small organisation than a menial in a large one.

You should be lucky in love, and happy, provided you put in the effort to make a comfortable home for yourself and those close to you. It is likely that you will have a love of pleasure, sport, music and literature. Life brings you many rewards, most of them as a direct result of your own efforts, although you may be luckier than average and ready to make the best of any situation.

Moon in Virgo

You are endowed with good mental abilities and a keen receptive memory, but you are never ostentatious or pretentious. Naturally quite reserved, you still have many friends, especially of the opposite sex. Marital relationships must be discussed carefully and worked at so that they remain harmonious, as personal attachments can be a problem if you do not give them your full attention.

Talented and persevering, you possess artistic qualities and are a good homemaker. Earning your honours through genuine merit, you work long and hard towards your objectives but show little pride in your achievements. Many short journeys will be undertaken in your life.

Moon in Libra

With the Moon in Libra you are naturally popular and make friends easily. People like you, probably more than you realise, you bring fun to a party and are a natural diplomat. For all its good points, Libra is not the most stable of astrological signs and, as a result, your emotions can be a little unstable too. Therefore, although the Moon in Libra is said to be good for love and marriage, your Sun sign and Rising sign will have an important effect on your emotional and loving qualities.

You must remember to relate to others in your decision-making. Co-operation is crucial because Libra represents the 'balance' of life that can only be achieved through harmonious relationships. Conformity is not easy for you because Libra, an Air sign, likes its independence.

Moon in Scorpio

Some people might call you pushy. In fact, all you really want to do is to live life to the full and protect yourself and your family from the pressures of life. Take care to avoid giving the impression of being sarcastic or impulsive and use your energies wisely and constructively.

You have great courage and you invariably achieve your goals by force of personality and sheer effort. You are fond of mystery and are good at predicting the outcome of situations and events. Travel experiences can be beneficial to you.

You may experience problems if you do not take time to examine your motives in a relationship, and also if you allow jealousy, always a feature of Scorpio, to cloud your judgement.

Moon in Sagittarius

The Moon in Sagittarius helps to make you a generous individual with humanitarian qualities and a kind heart. Restlessness may be intrinsic as your mind is seldom still. Perhaps because of this, you have a need for change that could lead you to several major moves during your adult life. You are not afraid to stand your ground when you know your judgement is right, you speak directly and have good intuition.

At work you are quick, efficient and versatile and so you make an ideal employee. You need work to be intellectually demanding and do not enjoy tedious routines.

In relationships, you anger quickly if faced with stupidity or deception, though you are just as quick to forgive and forget. Emotionally, there are times when your heart rules your head.

Moon in Capricorn

The Moon in Capricorn makes you popular and likely to come into the public eye in some way. The watery Moon is not entirely comfortable in the Earth sign of Capricorn and this may lead to some difficulties in the early years of life. An initial lack of creative ability and indecision must be overcome before the true qualities of patience and perseverance inherent in Capricorn can show through.

You have good administrative ability and are a capable worker, and if you are careful you can accumulate wealth. But you must be cautious and take professional advice in partnerships, as you are open to deception. You may be interested in social or welfare work, which suit your organisational skills and sympathy for others.

Moon in Aquarius

The Moon in Aquarius makes you an active and agreeable person with a friendly, easy-going nature. Sympathetic to the needs of others, you flourish in a laid-back atmosphere. You are broad-minded, fair and open to suggestion, although sometimes you have an unconventional quality which others can find hard to understand.

You are interested in the strange and curious, and in old articles and places. You enjoy trips to these places and gain much from them. Political, scientific and educational work interests you and you might choose a career in science or technology.

Money-wise, you make gains through innovation and concentration and Lunar Aquarians often tackle more than one job at a time. In love you are kind and honest.

Moon in Pisces

You have a kind, sympathetic nature, somewhat retiring at times, but you always take account of others' feelings and help when you can.

Personal relationships may be problematic, but as life goes on you can learn from your experiences and develop a better understanding of yourself and the world around you.

You have a fondness for travel, appreciate beauty and harmony and hate disorder and strife. You may be fond of literature and would make a good writer or speaker yourself. You have a creative imagination and may come across as an incurable romantic. You have strong intuition, maybe bordering on a mediumistic quality, which sets you apart from the mass. You may not be rich in cash terms, but your personal gifts are worth more than gold.

ARIES IN LOVE

Discover how compatible in love you are with people from the same and other signs of the zodiac. Five stars equals a match made in heaven!

Aries meets Aries

This could be be an all-or-nothing pairing. Both parties are from a dominant sign, so someone will have to be flexible in order to maintain personal harmony. Both know what they want out of life, and may have trouble overcoming any obstacles a relationship creates. This is a good physical pairing, with a chemistry that few other matches enjoy to the same level. Attitude is everything, but at least there is a mutual admiration that makes gazing at your partner like looking in the mirror. Star rating: ****

Aries meets Taurus

This is a match that has been known to work very well. Aries brings dynamism and ambition, while Taurus has the patience to see things through logically. Such complementary views work equally well in a relationship or in the office. There is mutual respect, but sometimes a lack of total understanding. The romantic needs of each are quite different, but both are still fulfilled. They can live easily in domestic harmony which is very important but, interestingly, Aries may be the loser in battles of will. Star rating: ***

Aries meets Gemini

Don't expect peace and harmony with this combination, although what comes along instead might make up for any disagreements. Gemini has a very fertile imagination, while Aries has the tenacity to make reality from fantasy. Combined, they have a sizzling relationship. There are times when both parties could explode with indignation and something has to give. But even if there are clashes, making them up will always be most enjoyable! Mutual financial success is likely in this match. Star rating: ****

Aries meets Cancer

A potentially one-sided pairing, it often appears that the Cancerian is brow-beaten by the far more dominant Arian. So much depends on the patience of the Cancerian individual, because if good psychology is present – who knows? But beware, Aries, you may find your partner too passive, and constantly having to take the lead can be wearing – even for you. A prolonged trial period would be advantageous, as the match could easily go either way. When it does work, though, this relationship is usually contented. Star rating: ***

Aries meets Leo

Stand by for action and make sure the house is sound-proof. Leo is a lofty idealist and there is always likely to be friction when two Fire signs meet. To compensate, there is much mutual admiration, together with a desire to please. Where there are shared incentives, the prognosis is good but it's important not to let little irritations blow up. Both signs want to have their own way and this is a sure cause of trouble. There might not be much patience here, but there is plenty of action. Star rating: *****

Aries meets Virgo

Neither of these signs really understands the other, and that could easily lead to a clash. Virgo is so pedantic, which will drive Aries up the wall, while Aries always wants to be moving on to the next objective, before Virgo is even settled with the last one. It will take time for these two to get to know each other, but this is a great business matching. If a personal relationship is seen in these terms then the prognosis can be good, but on the whole, this is not an inspiring match. Star rating: ***

Aries meets Libra

These signs are zodiac opposites which means a make-or-break situation. The match will either be a great success or a dismal failure. Why? Well Aries finds it difficult to understand the flighty Air-sign tendencies of Libra, whilst the natural balance of Libra contradicts the unorthodox Arian methods. Any flexibility will come from Libra, which may mean that things work out for a while, but Libra only has so much patience and it may eventually run out. In the end, Aries may be just too bossy for an independent but sensitive sign like Libra. Star rating: **

Aries meets Scorpio

There can be great affection here, even if the two zodiac signs are so very different. The common link is the planet Mars, which plays a part in both these natures. Although Aries is, outwardly, the most dominant, Scorpio people are among the most powerful to be found anywhere. This quiet determination is respected by Aries. Aries will satisfy the passionate side of Scorpio, particularly with instruction from Scorpio. There are mysteries here which will add spice to life. The few arguments that do occur are likely to be awe-inspiring. Star rating: ****

Aries meets Sagittarius

This can be one of the most favourable matches of them all. Both Aries and Sagittarius are Fire signs, which often leads to clashes of will, but this pair find a mutual understanding. Sagittarius helps Aries to develop a better sense of humour, while Aries teaches the Archer about consistency on the road to success. Some patience is called for on both sides, but these people have a natural liking for each other. Add this to growing love and you have a long-lasting combination that is hard to beat. Star rating: *****

Aries meets Capricorn

Capricorn works conscientiously to achieve its objectives and so can be the perfect companion for Aries. The Ram knows how to achieve but not how to consolidate, so the two signs have a great deal to offer one another practically. There may not be fireworks and it's sometimes doubtful how well they know each other, but it may not matter. Aries is outwardly hot but inwardly cool, whilst Capricorn can appear low key but be a furnace underneath. Such a pairing can gradually find contentment, though both parties may wonder how this is so. Star rating: ****

Aries meets Aquarius

Aquarius is an Air sign, and Air and Fire often work well together, but perhaps not in the case of Aries and Aquarius. The average Aquarian lives in what the Ram sees as a fantasy world, so without a sufficiently good meeting of minds, compromise may be lacking. Of course, almost anything is possible, and the dominant side of Aries could be trained by the devil-may-care attitude of Aquarius. There are meeting points but they are difficult to establish. However, given sufficient time and an open mind on both sides, a degree of happiness is possible. Star rating: **

Aries meets Pisces

Still waters run deep, and they don't come much deeper than Pisces. Although these signs share the same quadrant of the zodiac, they have little in common. Pisces is a dreamer, a romantic idealist with steady and spiritual goals. Aries needs to be on the move, and has very different ideals. It's hard to see how a relationship could develop because the outlook on life is so different but, with patience, especially from Aries, there is a chance that things might work out. Pisces needs incentive, and Aries may be the sign to offer it. Star rating: **

VENUS:
THE PLANET OF LOVE

If you look up at the sky around sunset or sunrise you will often see Venus in close attendance to the Sun. It is arguably one of the most beautiful sights of all and there is little wonder that historically it became associated with the goddess of love. But although Venus does play an important part in the way you view love and in the way others see you romantically, this is only one of the spheres of influence that it enjoys in your overall character.

Venus has a part to play in the more cultured side of your life and has much to do with your appreciation of art, literature, music and general creativity. Even the way you look is responsive to the part of the zodiac that Venus occupied at the start of your life, though this fact is also down to your Sun sign and Ascending sign. If, at the time you were born, Venus occupied one of the more gregarious zodiac signs, you will be more likely to wear your heart on your sleeve, as well as to be more attracted to entertainment, social gatherings and good company. If on the other hand Venus occupied a quiet zodiac sign at the time of your birth, you would tend to be more retiring and less willing to shine in public situations.

It's good to know what part the planet Venus plays in your life, for it can have a great bearing on the way you appear to the rest of the world and since we all have to mix with others, you can learn to make the very best of what Venus has to offer you.

One of the great complications in the past has always been trying to establish exactly what zodiac position Venus enjoyed when you were born, because the planet is notoriously difficult to track. However, I have solved that problem by creating a table that is exclusive to your Sun sign, which you will find on the following page.

Establishing your Venus sign could not be easier. Just look up the year of your birth on the page opposite and you will see a sign of the zodiac. This was the sign that Venus occupied in the period covered by your sign in that year. If Venus occupied more than one sign during the period, this is indicated by the date on which the sign changed, and the name of the new sign. For instance, if you were born in 1950, Venus was in Aquarius until the 7th April, after which time it was in Pisces. If you were born before 7th April your Venus sign is Aquarius, if you were born on or after 7th April, your Venus sign is Pisces. Once you have established the position of Venus at the time of your birth, you can then look in the pages which follow to see how this has a bearing on your life as a whole.

1912 PISCES / 14.4 ARIES
1913 TAURUS
1914 ARIES /14.4 TAURUS
1915 AQUARIUS / 1.4 PISCES
1916 TAURUS / 8.4 GEMINI
1917 PISCES / 28.3 ARIES
1918 AQUARIUS / 5.4 PISCES
1919 ARIES / 24.3 TAURUS
1920 PISCES / 14.4 ARIES
1921 TAURUS
1922 ARIES / 13.4 TAURUS
1923 AQUARIUS / 1.4 PISCES
1924 TAURUS / 6.4 GEMINI
1925 PISCES / 28.3 ARIES
1926 AQUARIUS / 6.4 PISCES
1927 ARIES / 24.3 TAURUS
1928 PISCES / 13.4 ARIES
1929 TAURUS / 20.4 ARIES
1930 ARIES / 13.4 TAURUS
1931 AQUARIUS / 31.3 PISCES
1932 TAURUS / 6.4 GEMINI
1933 PISCES / 27.3 ARIES
1934 AQUARIUS / 6.4 PISCES
1935 ARIES / 23.3 TAURUS
1936 PISCES / 13.4 ARIES
1937 TAURUS / 14.4 ARIES
1938 ARIES / 12.4 TAURUS
1939 AQUARIUS / 31.3 PISCES
1940 TAURUS / 5.4 GEMINI
1941 PISCES / 26.3 ARIES /
     20.4 TAURUS
1942 AQUARIUS / 7.4 PISCES
1943 ARIES / 23.3 TAURUS
1944 PISCES / 12.4 ARIES
1945 TAURUS / 8.4 ARIES
1946 ARIES / 12.4 TAURUS
1947 AQUARIUS / 30.3 PISCES
1948 TAURUS / 5.4 GEMINI
1949 PISCES / 25.3 ARIES /
     20.4 TAURUS
1950 AQUARIUS / 7.4 PISCES
1951 ARIES / 22.3 TAURUS
1952 PISCES / 12.4 ARIES
1953 TAURUS / 1.4 ARIES
1954 ARIES / 11.4 TAURUS
1955 AQUARIUS / 30.3 PISCES
1956 TAURUS / 4.4 GEMINI
1957 PISCES / 25.3 ARIES /
     19.4 TAURUS
1958 AQUARIUS / 8.4 PISCES
1959 ARIES / 22.3 TAURUS
1960 PISCES / 11.4 ARIES
1961 ARIES
1962 ARIES / 11.4 TAURUS

1963 AQUARIUS / 29.3 PISCES
1964 TAURUS / 4.4 GEMINI
1965 PISCES / 24.3 ARIES /
     19.4 TAURUS
1966 AQUARIUS / 8.4 PISCES
1967 TAURUS / 20.4 GEMINI
1968 PISCES / 10.4 ARIES
1969 ARIES
1970 ARIES / 10.4 TAURUS
1971 AQUARIUS / 29.3 PISCES
1972 TAURUS / 3.4 GEMINI
1973 PISCES / 24.3 ARIES /
     18.4 TAURUS
1974 AQUARIUS / 8.4 PISCES
1975 TAURUS / 19.4 GEMINI
1976 PISCES / 10.4 ARIES
1977 ARIES
1978 ARIES / 10.4 TAURUS
1979 AQUARIUS / 28.3 PISCES
1980 TAURUS / 3.4 GEMINI
1981 PISCES / 23.3 ARIES /
     18.4 TAURUS
1982 AQUARIUS / 9.4 PISCES
1983 TAURUS / 19.4 GEMINI
1984 PISCES / 9.4 ARIES
1985 ARIES
1986 ARIES / 9.4 TAURUS
1987 AQUARIUS / 28.3 PISCES
1988 TAURUS / 2.4 GEMINI
1989 PISCES / 23.3 ARIES /
     17.4 TAURUS
1990 AQUARIUS / 9.4 PISCES
1991 TAURUS / 18.4 GEMINI
1992 PISCES / 9.4 ARIES
1993 ARIES
1994 ARIES / 9.4 TAURUS
1995 AQUARIUS / 27.3 PISCES
1996 TAURUS / 2.4 GEMINI
1997 PISCES / 22.3 ARIES /
     17.4 TAURUS
1998 AQUARIUS / 9.4 PISCES
1999 TAURUS / 18.4 GEMINI
2000 PISCES / 9.4 ARIES
2001 ARIES
2002 ARIES / 7.4 TAURUS
2003 AQUARIUS / 27.3 PISCES
2004 TAURUS / 1.4 GEMINI
2005 PISCES/22.3 ARIES
2006 AQUARIUS / 7.4 PISCES
2007 TAURUS / 16.4 GEMINI
2008 PISCES / 9.4 ARIES
2009 ARIES
2010 ARIES / 7.4 TAURUS

VENUS THROUGH THE ZODIAC SIGNS

Venus in Aries

Amongst other things, the position of Venus in Aries indicates a fondness for travel, music and all creative pursuits. Your nature tends to be affectionate and you would try not to create confusion or difficulty for others if it could be avoided. Many people with this planetary position have a great love of the theatre, and mental stimulation is of the greatest importance. Early romantic attachments are common with Venus in Aries, so it is very important to establish a genuine sense of romantic continuity. Early marriage is not recommended, especially if it is based on sympathy. You may give your heart a little too readily on occasions.

Venus in Taurus

You are capable of very deep feelings and your emotions tend to last for a very long time. This makes you a trusting partner and lover, whose constancy is second to none. In life you are precise and careful and always try to do things the right way. Although this means an ordered life, which you are comfortable with, it can also lead you to be rather too fussy for your own good. Despite your pleasant nature, you are very fixed in your opinions and quite able to speak your mind. Others are attracted to you and historical astrologers always quoted this position of Venus as being very fortunate in terms of marriage. However, if you find yourself involved in a failed relationship, it could take you a long time to trust again.

Venus in Gemini

As with all associations related to Gemini, you tend to be quite versatile, anxious for change and intelligent in your dealings with the world at large. You may gain money from more than one source but you are equally good at spending it. There is an inference here that you are a good communicator, via either the written or the spoken word, and you love to be in the company of interesting people. Always on the look-out for culture, you may also be very fond of music, and love to indulge the curious and cultured side of your nature. In romance you tend to have more than one relationship and could find yourself associated with someone who has previously been a friend or even a distant relative.

Venus in Cancer

You often stay close to home because you are very fond of family and enjoy many of your most treasured moments when you are with those you love. Being naturally sympathetic, you will always do anything you can to support those around you, even people you hardly know at all. This charitable side of your nature is your most noticeable trait and is one of the reasons why others are naturally so fond of you. Being receptive and in some cases even psychic, you can see through to the soul of most of those with whom you come into contact. You may not commence too many romantic attachments but when you do give your heart, it tends to be unconditionally.

Venus in Leo

It must become quickly obvious to almost anyone you meet that you are kind, sympathetic and yet determined enough to stand up for anyone or anything that is truly important to you. Bright and sunny, you warm the world with your natural enthusiasm and would rarely do anything to hurt those around you, or at least not intentionally. In romance you are ardent and sincere, though some may find your style just a little overpowering. Gains come through your contacts with other people and this could be especially true with regard to romance, for love and money often come hand in hand for those who were born with Venus in Leo. People claim to understand you, though you are more complex than you seem.

Venus in Virgo

Your nature could well be fairly quiet no matter what your Sun sign might be, though this fact often manifests itself as an inner peace and would not prevent you from being basically sociable. Some delays and even the odd disappointment in love cannot be ruled out with this planetary position, though it's a fact that you will usually find the happiness you look for in the end. Catapulting yourself into romantic entanglements that you know to be rather ill-advised is not sensible, and it would be better to wait before you committed yourself exclusively to any one person. It is the essence of your nature to serve the world at large and through doing so it is possible that you will attract money at some stage in your life.

Venus in Libra

Venus is very comfortable in Libra and bestows upon those people who have this planetary position a particular sort of kindness that is easy to recognise. This is a very good position for all sorts of friendships and also for romantic attachments that usually bring much joy into your life. Few individuals with Venus in Libra would avoid marriage and since you are capable of great depths of love, it is likely that you will find a contented personal life. You like to mix with people of integrity and intelligence but don't take kindly to scruffy surroundings or work that means getting your hands too dirty. Careful speculation, good business dealings and money through marriage all seem fairly likely.

Venus in Scorpio

You are quite open and tend to spend money quite freely, even on those occasions when you don't have very much. Although your intentions are always good, there are times when you get yourself in to the odd scrape and this can be particularly true when it comes to romance, which you may come to late or from a rather unexpected direction. Certainly you have the power to be happy and to make others contented on the way, but you find the odd stumbling block on your journey through life and it could seem that you have to work harder than those around you. As a result of this, you gain a much deeper understanding of the true value of personal happiness than many people ever do, and are likely to achieve true contentment in the end.

Venus in Sagittarius

You are lighthearted, cheerful and always able to see the funny side of any situation. These facts enhance your popularity, which is especially high with members of the opposite sex. You should never have to look too far to find romantic interest in your life, though it is just possible that you might be too willing to commit yourself before you are certain that the person in question is right for you. Part of the problem here extends to other areas of life too. The fact is that you like variety in everything and so can tire of situations that fail to offer it. All the same, if you choose wisely and learn to understand your restless side, then great happiness can be yours.

Venus in Capricorn

The most notable trait that comes from Venus in this position is that it makes you trustworthy and able to take on all sorts of responsibilities in life. People are instinctively fond of you and love you all the more because you are always ready to help those who are in any form of need. Social and business popularity can be yours and there is a magnetic quality to your nature that is particularly attractive in a romantic sense. Anyone who wants a partner for a lover, a spouse and a good friend too would almost certainly look in your direction. Constancy is the hallmark of your nature and unfaithfulness would go right against the grain. You might sometimes be a little too trusting.

Venus in Aquarius

This location of Venus offers a fondness for travel and a desire to try out something new at every possible opportunity. You are extremely easy to get along with and tend to have many friends from varied backgrounds, classes and inclinations. You like to live a distinct sort of life and gain a great deal from moving about, both in a career sense and with regard to your home. It is not out of the question that you could form a romantic attachment to someone who comes from far away or be attracted to a person of a distinctly artistic and original nature. What you cannot stand is jealousy, for you have friends of both sexes and would want to keep things that way.

Venus in Pisces

The first thing people tend to notice about you is your wonderful, warm smile. Being very charitable by nature you will do anything to help others, even if you don't know them well. Much of your life may be spent sorting out situations for other people, but it is very important to feel that you are living for yourself too. In the main, you remain cheerful, and tend to be quite attractive to members of the opposite sex. Where romantic attachments are concerned, you could be drawn to people who are significantly older or younger than yourself or to someone with a unique career or point of view. It might be best for you to avoid marrying whilst you are still very young.

THE ASTRAL DIARY

HOW THE DIAGRAMS WORK

Through the picture diagrams in the Astral Diary I want to help you to plot your year. With them you can see where the positive and negative aspects will be found in each month. To make the most of them, all you have to do is remember where and when!

Let me show you how they work ...

THE MONTH AT A GLANCE

Just as there are twelve separate zodiac signs, so astrologers believe that each sign has twelve separate aspects to life. Each of the twelve segments relates to a different personal aspect. I list them all every month so that their meanings are always clear.

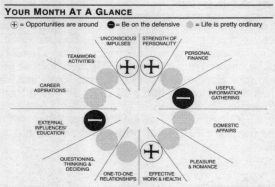

YOUR MONTH AT A GLANCE

⊕ = Opportunities are around　⊖ = Be on the defensive　⬤ = Life is pretty ordinary

UNCONSCIOUS IMPULSES

STRENGTH OF PERSONALITY

TEAMWORK ACTIVITIES

PERSONAL FINANCE

CAREER ASPIRATIONS

USEFUL INFORMATION GATHERING

EXTERNAL INFLUENCES/ EDUCATION

DOMESTIC AFFAIRS

QUESTIONING, THINKING & DECIDING

PLEASURE & ROMANCE

ONE-TO-ONE RELATIONSHIPS

EFFECTIVE WORK & HEALTH

I have designed this chart to show you how and when these twelve different aspects are being influenced throughout the year. When there is a shaded circle, nothing out of the ordinary is to be expected. However, when a circle turns white with a plus sign, the influence is positive. Where the circle is black with a minus sign, it is a negative.

YOUR ENERGY RHYTHM CHART

On the opposite page is a picture diagram in which I am linking your zodiac group to the rhythm of the Moon. In doing this I have calculated when you will be gaining strength from its influence and equally when you may be weakened by it.

If you think of yourself as being like the tides of the ocean then you may understand how your own energies must also rise and fall. And if you understand how it works and when it is working, then you can better organise your activities to achieve more and get things done more easily.

YOUR ENERGY RHYTHM CHART

Increasing in energy as the month goes on

At your best on 20th–21st

HIGH 20TH–21ST

Energy falling again from the 23rd

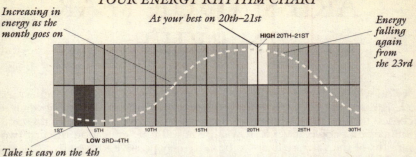

1ST · 5TH · 10TH · 15TH · 20TH · 25TH · 30TH

LOW 3RD–4TH

Take it easy on the 4th

MOVING PICTURE SCREEN
Love, money, career and vitality measured every week

The diagram at the end of each week is designed to be informative and fun. The arrows move up and down the scale to give you an idea of the strength of your opportunities in each area. If LOVE stands at plus 4, then get out and put yourself about because things are going your way in romance! The further down the arrow goes, the weaker the opportunities. Do note that the diagram is an overall view of your astrological aspects and therefore reflects a trend which may not concur with every day in that cycle.

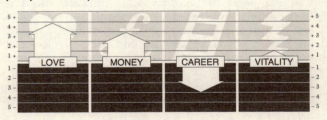

LOVE   MONEY   CAREER   VITALITY

AND FINALLY:

am . . . .

pm . . . .

The two lines that are left blank in each daily entry of the Astral Diary are for your own personal use. You may find them ideal for keeping a check on birthdays or appointments, though it could be an idea to make notes from the astrological trends and diagrams a few weeks in advance. Some of the lines are marked with a key, which indicates the working of astrological cycles in your life. Look out for them each week as they are the best days to take action or make decisions. The daily text tells you which area of your life to focus on.

☿ = Mercury is retrograde on that day.

ARIES: YOUR YEAR IN BRIEF

You will notice a time of both gains and losses as 2010 gets underway. January and February offer you new commitments, especially when it comes to romance, and you could also be making new friends and influencing people at work. If you are in full-time education the first two months of the year are likely to be extremely positive for you.

March and April bring better times in terms of finances, if only because you are taking more responsibility for your spending, and you will also be in a better position to save money than has been the case over the last few months. When it comes to friendship you are likely to be on top form this year, and once again you manage to meet new people and to form what should be quite lasting bonds.

With the early summer you are at your best socially and keen to make a good impression on just about anyone you meet. At work you can make significant progress and have a positive influence on people who have the power to help you. You look towards the future with greater hope than ever and will be doing your best to support those who are not as confident as you tend to be. May and June are also going to be potentially good for travel.

July and August will find you moving about freely, anxious to make a good impression wherever you go and probably less testy than is sometimes the case for Aries individuals. Your powers of communication are especially good and there are gains to be made when it comes to money. Good luck follows you around, so do what you can to make the best of it. Travel is once again on the agenda throughout this two-month period.

With the autumn you might be slightly quieter. September and October see you withdrawing into yourself more than has been the case earlier in the year and you do whatever you can to stay out of the limelight, especially in September. Popularity cannot be avoided and if you really think about it you are happiest when at the centre of things. Take every opportunity to address financial matters and contracts during the month of October.

The last two months of the year, November and December, will find you on top form again. You are likely to be doing much of the planning that takes place for festivities, sometimes long before Christmas comes along. Love is high on your agenda and you actively seek out new relationships or else do what you can to support existing attachments. It ought to be a happy and generally carefree end to the year.

January
2010

YOUR MONTH AT A GLANCE

⊕ = Opportunities are around　⊖ = Be on the defensive　● = Life is pretty ordinary

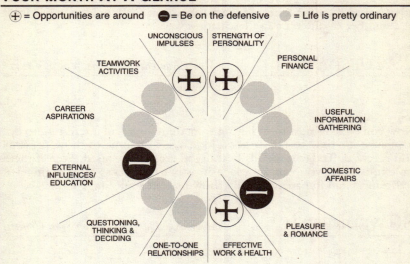

JANUARY HIGHS AND LOWS

Here I show you how the rhythms of the Moon will affect you this month. Like the tide, your energies and abilities will rise and fall with its pattern. When it is above the centre line, go for it, when it is below, you should be resting.

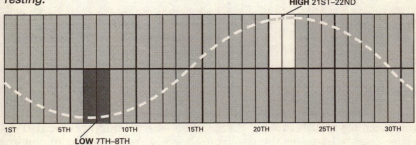

HIGH 21ST–22ND

LOW 7TH–8TH

41

28 MONDAY
Moon Age Day 12   Moon Sign Taurus

am . . . .

pm . . . .
You will be at your best today when you are involved with groups of people, or organisations that have aims and objectives that appeal specifically to you. There is something quite political about Aries just now, not to mention a deeply charitable streak that could manifest itself in a number of different and fascinating ways.

29 TUESDAY
Moon Age Day 13   Moon Sign Taurus

am . . . .

pm . . . .
Now you benefit most from having something new and interesting to do, so maybe it's time to take a good look again at some of those presents you received. Today responds best if you are very focused, even if there isn't too much you can approach in a practical sense. Just a tinge of restlessness and impatience could show itself at some stage today.

30 WEDNESDAY
Moon Age Day 14   Moon Sign Gemini

am . . . .

pm . . . .
Material pleasures are now to the fore, because the more thoughtful phase of the pre-Christmas days is now well out of the way. Sporting activities might appeal as well, and it is possible you will be on the way to the gym or else finding some large hill to climb. Aries is on the move again.

31 THURSDAY
Moon Age Day 15   Moon Sign Gemini

am . . . .

pm . . . .
There are some added responsibilities about today and with the year-end parties in view that probably isn't too surprising. Don't be too quick to volunteer for things though because you might find your social style being cramped later in the day. You always look forward to midnight, because that's the start of a whole new ball game.

1 FRIDAY   ☿   *Moon Age Day 16   Moon Sign Cancer*

am . . . .

pm . . . .
On the first day of the year you should be raring to go, though the rest of the world could take some time catching up. If people you know well are behaving in a less than typical way, you may have to make allowance for their attitude and actions. Try to perfect a plan now that will see you making significant progress later.

2 SATURDAY   ☿   *Moon Age Day 17   Moon Sign Cancer*

am . . . .

pm . . . .
It could be somewhat difficult today following rules and regulations that someone else is setting for you. The truth is that you have your own way of doing things and you might not take too kindly to being told how to behave. It would be best to avoid confrontation and to toe the line, at least for the next day or two.

3 SUNDAY   ☿   *Moon Age Day 18   Moon Sign Leo*

am . . . .

pm . . . .
A standard response to romantic matters might not work for the moment and it is clear that in your relationships with certain other people you will have to think on your feet. Attitude is very important at work, and you will need to be quite definite when it comes to organising your life for the weeks and months that lie ahead.

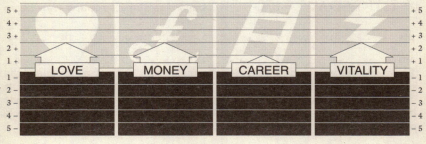

4 MONDAY   ☿   *Moon Age Day 19   Moon Sign Leo*

am . . . .

pm . . . .
Your need to be the centre of attention is in evidence to start the year.
The more forceful side of Aries is showing, indicating that you won't take
kindly to any sort of opposition. Welcoming people from the past back
into your life is fine, but not everything they bring with them is welcome,
so it's worth paying close attention.

5 TUESDAY   ☿   *Moon Age Day 20   Moon Sign Virgo*

am . . . .

pm . . . .
Give and take are important factors today, and with some slightly adverse
planetary trends you need to be especially careful not to upset those you
rely on the most. Once again your dominant side is highlighted, which
can work well in some circumstances, though not in all. Stand up for
others rather than for yourself.

6 WEDNESDAY   ☿   *Moon Age Day 21   Moon Sign Virgo*

am . . . .

pm . . . .
Routines should suit you well today, though you should be on fine form
romantically and have what it takes to turn heads when in company. Even
if others are happy to have a quiet January, this may not be the case for
you. Aries is always on the go and finds it difficult to understand people
who are feeling at all lazy.

7 THURSDAY   ☿   *Moon Age Day 22   Moon Sign Libra*

am . . . .

pm . . . .
The decisions of others could now take the wind out of your sails. This
situation is not helped by the lunar low, that period of the month when
the Moon is in your opposite zodiac sign. Your best approach is to avoid
getting involved in any grand new deals for the moment, because it's
possible that not everyone around you is honest.

8 FRIDAY ☿ *Moon Age Day 23 Moon Sign Libra*

am . . . .

pm . . . .
Why not lower your sights and dig in for a day or two? This would be an ideal way of dealing with the lunar low. As long as you treat this period as a time for rest and reflection, you can make sure all is well. What you can't afford at the moment is to put yourself out on any ledge or to insist that you have the answer to everything.

9 SATURDAY ☿ *Moon Age Day 24 Moon Sign Scorpio*

am . . . .

pm . . . .
It is possible that you will be tempted to change your mind regarding an issue that has been close to your heart for some time. Maybe you should leave things the way they are for the moment. The only thing you can be sure about today is that you are not certain about anything. Good advice from friends should not be ignored.

10 SUNDAY ☿ *Moon Age Day 25 Moon Sign Scorpio*

am . . . .

pm . . . .
Though getting along with others should prove to be generally easy, you might find it difficult to get to know some people in the way you would wish.. You can't expect everyone to respond to your charm, even if you are handing it out by the ladle! Bear in mind that it's unusual to be liked by absolutely everyone.

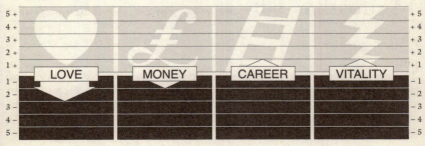

11 MONDAY   ☿   *Moon Age Day 26   Moon Sign Sagittarius*

am . . . .

pm . . . .
A time of greater mental energy is at hand, so you can make the start of
this new working week quite dynamic. Even if you don't find everyone
to be equally co-operative at this time, you do have what it takes to build
a good team spirit, which extends far into the day. Socially speaking the
potential is especially good.

12 TUESDAY   ☿   *Moon Age Day 27   Moon Sign Sagittarius*

am . . . .

pm . . . .
Peace and quiet may be hard to achieve at home right now. Everyone has
their own particular point of view and each might be voicing their version
at the same time. Life can be a madhouse, in which you seem to be little
more than a casual observer. A day to simply laugh at the situation and
do what is necessary to get by.

13 WEDNESDAY   ☿   *Moon Age Day 28   Moon Sign Sagittarius*

am . . . .

pm . . . .
In terms of your career, a favoured plan of action may not yield the
results you would wish. Instead of giving up altogether, simply look at
things afresh and make some modifications. Although goals and
ambitions may seem a long way off, with a little patience you can start an
important personal journey that will last for months.

14 THURSDAY   ☿   *Moon Age Day 29   Moon Sign Capricorn*

am . . . .

pm . . . .
The art of good conversation is something that isn't lost on you, and
particularly not at present. It's a good idea to check and recheck your
actions today, especially at work. Creating a good impression is what it's
all about. Some Aries subjects might now be considering a change of
occupation.

15 FRIDAY ☿ *Moon Age Day 0 Moon Sign Capricorn*

am . . . .

pm . . . .
You have what it takes to bring harmony to romance and personal relationships today, and it is in the sphere of personal attachments that you can gain most. You needn't let the heavy demands of your partner bother you at present. The time is right to ring the changes in a social sense, especially this evening.

16 SATURDAY ☿ *Moon Age Day 1 Moon Sign Aquarius*

am . . . .

pm . . . .
Don't miss any opportunity to make gains in the material world. While fortune favours your efforts you need to demonstrate exactly what you are made of and to push forward as progressively as you can. This is a time to show the most positive qualities of your zodiac sign to everyone, and wow, are you positive!

17 SUNDAY *Moon Age Day 2 Moon Sign Aquarius*

am . . . .

pm . . . .
Thanks to the beneficial romantic advantages that are around you today, personal attachments matter a great deal. Trends favour more time spent in the company of your partner and in dealing with the general needs and wants of family members. The urge to travel is strongly highlighted at present.

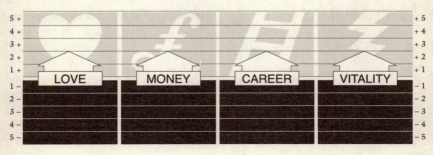

18 MONDAY   *Moon Age Day 3   Moon Sign Aquarius*

am . . . .

pm . . . .
If there is something missing on this particular Monday, it's up to you to find what it is and put it right. For the moment you become a great lover of mystery and so shouldn't mind delving a little into certain aspects of life. In terms of entertainment you can be very flexible at this stage, so pep up your life as much as possible!

19 TUESDAY   *Moon Age Day 4   Moon Sign Pisces*

am . . . .

pm . . . .
There could be a few small setbacks on the work front today, and if so you will need to act and react quickly to changing circumstances. Give and take is important when dealing with loved ones, particularly if they are awkward to cope with. Socially speaking you might be on better form towards the end of the day, so why not go out?

20 WEDNESDAY   *Moon Age Day 5   Moon Sign Pisces*

am . . . .

pm . . . .
For the moment you should be making the most of what the practical world has to offer. Beware of becoming touchy and of taking offence where none is intended, especially if not everyone is easy to get on with. You might decide to tackle some important jobs around the house, and you needn't let the winter put you off.

21 THURSDAY   *Moon Age Day 6   Moon Sign Aries*

am . . . .

pm . . . .
Today the Moon returns to your own zodiac sign of Aries, offering high levels of both mental and physical energy. You are now better able to burn the candle at both ends. There are possible gains through the part others play in your life, and in social or business associations you can display yourself as inspirational and powerful.

22 FRIDAY *Moon Age Day 7   Moon Sign Aries*

am . . . .

pm . . . .
In a personal or indeed a professional sense, you should definitely have
the edge now. What you want at the moment is to be in charge of your
own life, and woe betide anyone who tries to prevent this. In reality, you
can get most of those you encounter on your side and should attract the
strong support of relatives and friends.

23 SATURDAY *Moon Age Day 8   Moon Sign Aries*

am . . . .

pm . . . .
Promising developments on the financial front may prompt you to spend
somewhat more freely than has been the case of late. If you fancy the odd
flutter this ought to be possible, and there is no reason to fear the natural
interaction you are having with the world at large. Be prepared to give
your time freely to relatives or deserving friends.

24 SUNDAY *Moon Age Day 9   Moon Sign Taurus*

am . . . .

pm . . . .
Domestic matters might seem something of a trial to you today, making
it rather difficult for you to achieve the level of progress you might wish
in a practical or professional sense. All the same, it won't do you any
harm to take things steady for a few hours, or to spend more time with
loved ones. Get a grip on your finances.

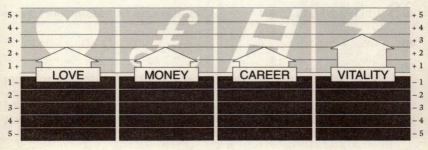

25 MONDAY
Moon Age Day 10   Moon Sign Taurus

am . . . .

pm . . . .
This might well be a good day to go travelling. Any restlessness within your nature can probably be helped by moving about. Even small journeys would suit you better than staying put. Mentally speaking you have what it takes to be on top form and can make sure you aren't duped today by anyone, no matter how clever they are.

26 TUESDAY
Moon Age Day 11   Moon Sign Gemini

am . . . .

pm . . . .
Today could turn out to be especially good for problem solving. If you have your clever head on, you can use it to fathom out all sorts of details that would normally prove to be very difficult. Even if not everyone is on your side now, you should be able to glean the support you need from the people who matter the most.

27 WEDNESDAY
Moon Age Day 12   Moon Sign Gemini

am . . . .

pm . . . .
Intimate relationships are potentially the most rewarding area of your life right now. Trends assist you to say just the right things to please people and to attract a warm and helpful response from friends. Are strangers difficult to deal with? That's a small price to pay on what should otherwise be a good mixing day.

28 THURSDAY
Moon Age Day 13   Moon Sign Cancer

am . . . .

pm . . . .
The chance to get some leisure time in is now at hand. This may not really sound like you, but even Aries needs to have a break on occasions. On the other hand, the more you get done today, the better you will be placed to enjoy what is on offer when the weekend arrives. The choice is yours, but whatever you decide, don't overwork!

29 FRIDAY
Moon Age Day 14   Moon Sign Cancer

am . . . .

pm . . . .
There is a possibility that you may feel let down by a friend. If so, your best response is to let them know how you feel. You won't get very far beating about the bush. There are times when it is sensible to bite your lip, but this isn't one of them. In any case, you can manage to remain diplomatic on the way, and that is sensible.

30 SATURDAY
Moon Age Day 15   Moon Sign Leo

am . . . .

pm . . . .
Today offers you the chance to capitalise on any new opportunity that comes along. Do what you can to get specific jobs out of the way, particularly if you have been making changes at home. Socially you need the cut and thrust of as many different sorts of individuals as you can possibly manage on this particular Saturday.

31 SUNDAY
Moon Age Day 16   Moon Sign Leo

am . . . .

pm . . . .
All in all you can make this a fairly successful and generally progressive day, after what may have been a slightly slower period. Broadening your horizons should not be too difficult, and with a Sunday in front of you during which it is possible to please yourself, you can afford to take some time out to do whatever takes your fancy.

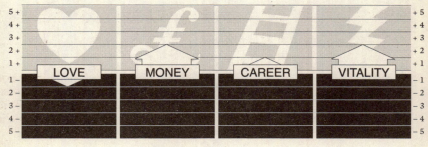

February 2010

YOUR MONTH AT A GLANCE

⊕ = Opportunities are around ⊖ = Be on the defensive ⬤ = Life is pretty ordinary

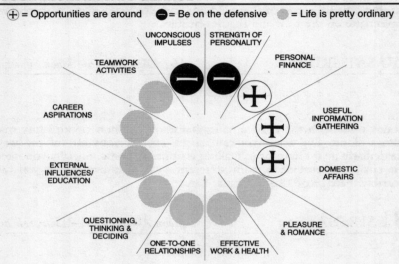

UNCONSCIOUS IMPULSES

STRENGTH OF PERSONALITY

PERSONAL FINANCE

TEAMWORK ACTIVITIES

CAREER ASPIRATIONS

USEFUL INFORMATION GATHERING

EXTERNAL INFLUENCES/ EDUCATION

DOMESTIC AFFAIRS

QUESTIONING, THINKING & DECIDING

PLEASURE & ROMANCE

ONE-TO-ONE RELATIONSHIPS

EFFECTIVE WORK & HEALTH

FEBRUARY HIGHS AND LOWS

Here I show you how the rhythms of the Moon will affect you this month. Like the tide, your energies and abilities will rise and fall with its pattern. When it is above the centre line, go for it, when it is below, you should be resting.

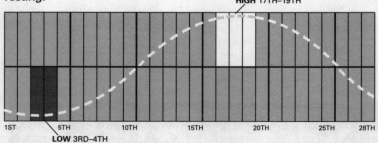

HIGH 17TH–19TH

LOW 3RD–4TH

1ST 5TH 10TH 15TH 20TH 25TH 28TH

1 MONDAY
Moon Age Day 17   Moon Sign Virgo

am . . . .

pm . . . .
This is a time when you have scope to profit from practical matters. You should thrive on work at the moment, and needn't let yourself be held back by anyone or anything. A day to display yourself to the world as a fairly typical Aries subject should, and though not at your absolute luckiest just now you can make great headway.

2 TUESDAY
Moon Age Day 18   Moon Sign Virgo

am . . . .

pm . . . .
You can afford to be generally good-natured for the moment and tend to get on well with just about anyone. This is especially true in the case of colleagues, even if some family members seem to be rubbing you up the wrong way. From a social point of view you can now find new methods to increase your popularity no end.

3 WEDNESDAY
Moon Age Day 19   Moon Sign Libra

am . . . .

pm . . . .
Today is the start of the lunar low, and that means you will have to be slightly more careful in the way you approach situations. Your luck is not to the fore, so games of chance are best avoided. Likewise it would be sensible to only take on tasks you know you could do in your sleep. Leave the outrageous behaviour until later!

4 THURSDAY
Moon Age Day 20   Moon Sign Libra

am . . . .

pm . . . .
Some opportunities may be lost, but you should look for chances to catch up with certain plans later on. What remains important for the moment is to consolidate your efforts and to concentrate in areas where success is more or less guaranteed. The more you stick your neck out today, the greater is the chance that you will make mistakes.

5 FRIDAY
Moon Age Day 21   Moon Sign Scorpio

am . . . .

pm . . . .
Today can be both pleasant and fun. Mars is in your solar fifth house, encouraging you to be well disposed to friends, as well as being flavour of the month amongst colleagues. You show a strong desire to have a good time and can maintain this across the coming weekend. It's time to dispel any difficulties caused by the lunar low.

6 SATURDAY
Moon Age Day 22   Moon Sign Scorpio

am . . . .

pm . . . .
When it comes to friendships, trends allow you to be both optimistic and confident now. What a great day this would be for getting out of the house and doing something completely different. Sporting Aries subjects might decide to pit themselves against others, but any competition should be good-natured. Life offers its own rewards.

7 SUNDAY
Moon Age Day 23   Moon Sign Scorpio

am . . . .

pm . . . .
Venus is now in your solar eleventh house, a good position for the planet of love when it comes to your social life. You have what it takes to be sympathetic towards other people who are having a hard time or who are not as naturally confident as you are. You may be drawn towards charitable causes today and can offer great help.

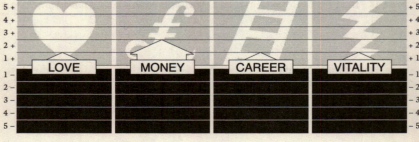

8 MONDAY
Moon Age Day 24   Moon Sign Sagittarius

am ....

pm ....
Mars in particular remains in a good position to help you to show a sociable and friendly face to the world at large. You can ensure people want to have you around and can be the life and soul of any situation by being both warm and funny. Anyone who has been scared of you in the past should have nothing to fear now.

9 TUESDAY
Moon Age Day 25   Moon Sign Sagittarius

am ....

pm ....
It is time to focus on some of your obligations and to get round to doing those things you might have been putting off for quite some time. You can console yourself with the thought that there isn't really that much you will be missing just now. The weather is probably unlikely to inspire you or to invite you out into the world.

10 WEDNESDAY
Moon Age Day 26   Moon Sign Capricorn

am ....

pm ....
The present position of Venus will encourage you out into the open, and even if being on display is not too much of a problem, there are moments when you could feel slightly vulnerable. If this turns out to be the case it is because a part of your deeper, more secret nature is laid bare. Sometimes it's good to show the real you.

11 THURSDAY
Moon Age Day 27   Moon Sign Capricorn

am ....

pm ....
You would prefer nothing to hold you back at the moment, but there isn't anything especially surprising about that for an Aries subject. Financial matters could require a little extra thought, and there is a slight chance that you could lose out to a competitor unless you keep your thinking head on. Don't rise to anyone else's bait.

12 FRIDAY
Moon Age Day 28   Moon Sign Aquarius

am . . . .

pm . . . .
A sort of lively sociability prevails at the moment. Little Mercury is in a good position to help you make the most of happy conversations and it appears that you can say exactly the right thing when it matters the most. You can persuade those around you to be supportive, and to do what they can to make you feel at ease.

13 SATURDAY
Moon Age Day 29   Moon Sign Aquarius

am . . . .

pm . . . .
The Sun is now in your solar eleventh house, which encourages a warm and friendly approach towards just about anyone. All the same there may be individuals who seem to know exactly how to rub you up the wrong way, and the best thing to do about such people today is to stay away from them. Stick to those who fascinate you.

14 SUNDAY
Moon Age Day 0   Moon Sign Aquarius

am . . . .

pm . . . .
Romantic idealism takes over as Venus moves into your solar twelfth house. There could well be a fairly dreamy quality to the next few weeks, and we can only hope that life lives up to your personal expectations of it. One thing is for certain – you have a heightened sensitivity to the needs of others, though perhaps not everyone.

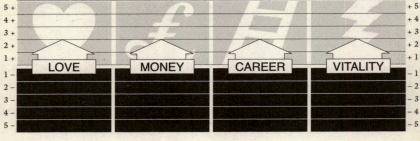

15 MONDAY

Moon Age Day 1   Moon Sign Pisces

am ....

pm ....
There are signs of a slightly too domineering approach today, prompting you to find ways and means to irritate some of the people on whom you have to rely. A more laid-back attitude would help, and that becomes more possible as the day advances. Ahead of the lunar high you can begin to develop a more dream-like quality.

16 TUESDAY

Moon Age Day 2   Moon Sign Pisces

am ....

pm ....
In romantic matters the time is now right to follow your heart. It's worth finding moments to reflect on the direction your life is presently taking and remaining open to the sound advice of your friends. By tomorrow you can begin to speed things up, but for the moment you should be quite happy to watch, wait and carefully plan.

17 WEDNESDAY

Moon Age Day 3   Moon Sign Aries

am ....

pm ....
Getting your own way should be easier today. The lunar high should find you anxious to get on and keen to show the world at large how much you know. If you get Lady Luck on your side you can afford to take a few more chances than might normally be the case. All you really need to avoid today is being too bossy or domineering.

18 THURSDAY

Moon Age Day 4   Moon Sign Aries

am ....

pm ....
Confidence remains quite high, assisting you to deal with the more important matters that are at the top of your agenda. By all means give yourself a pat on the back for successes, but you needn't gloat, because there is always more you can achieve. In most situations you can be the one who makes the running today and tomorrow.

19 FRIDAY

Moon Age Day 5   Moon Sign Aries

am . . . .

pm . . . .

At the start of today the Moon remains in your own zodiac sign of Aries. That means you can still be in charge and quite able to make any decisions that prove to be necessary. Watch out later for little accidents or mishaps that could stop you in your tracks, and also do what you can to show support for less motivated friends.

20 SATURDAY

Moon Age Day 6   Moon Sign Taurus

am . . . .

pm . . . .

Present planetary influences can quicken your intellect and make it possible for you to think on your feet. There is nothing especially surprising about this for the average Aries subject, but you can make others marvel at your ability to get everything right first time. This is a weekend that can offer much in the way of social interaction.

21 SUNDAY

Moon Age Day 7   Moon Sign Taurus

am . . . .

pm . . . .

The Sun is now in your solar twelfth house and this tends to strengthen your psychic abilities. Your real forte at the moment lies in using your imagination to the full because in many respects if you can dream it right now, you can probably do it as well. There are gains to be made from family members and even close friends.

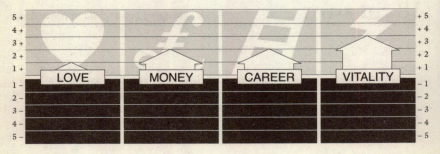

22 MONDAY
Moon Age Day 8   Moon Sign Gemini

am . . . .

pm . . . .
Now you can show your strong personal magnetism and your desire to get on the right side of people you haven't always seen eye to eye with in the past. Today responds best if you are more understanding and less inclined to dominate situations. If you are approachable, there is a good chance you will be making new friends around now.

23 TUESDAY
Moon Age Day 9   Moon Sign Gemini

am . . . .

pm . . . .
A period of increased concern for the success of others is now at hand. Instead of going solely for your own objectives, the position of the Sun in your solar chart allows you to take a back seat, whilst at the same time showing significant support for loved ones. Even colleagues can benefit from your present charitable state of mind.

24 WEDNESDAY
Moon Age Day 10   Moon Sign Cancer

am . . . .

pm . . . .
With both the Sun and Venus in your twelfth house you could well be about as dreamy as Aries ever gets. If you let the true warmth of your nature shine out like the sun, you have what it takes to increase your popularity no end. Don't waste any opportunity to do something kind, because even strangers deserve your support.

25 THURSDAY
Moon Age Day 11   Moon Sign Cancer

am . . . .

pm . . . .
You now have scope to express yourself in ways that will surprise even those who think they know you very well. Unbidden kindnesses become the hallmark of your nature, and the focus is on expressing yourself in positive terms, whoever you are mixing with. Even the practical side of your nature can be turned towards good deeds.

26 FRIDAY
Moon Age Day 12   Moon Sign Cancer

am . . . .

pm . . . .
In relationships with loved ones the present position of the Moon influences you greatly. Your romantic spirit is boosted, assisting you to find the right words to let your partner know exactly how you feel. In a social sense the weekend starts here for many Aries subjects, so you may not be too committed to your work today!

27 SATURDAY
Moon Age Day 13   Moon Sign Leo

am . . . .

pm . . . .
This could be a time of great insight into yourself and how you fit into the world at large. All the twelfth-house influences that surround you at the moment help you to be perceptive and to get on with almost anyone. This is especially the case if you understand what makes them tick. Try to maintain this ability in the days ahead.

28 SUNDAY
Moon Age Day 14   Moon Sign Leo

am . . . .

pm . . . .
What should really appeal to you now is the thought that whatever you are doing is useful. On the other hand, you may not take kindly to doing the same old things time and again and can soon become bored by routines. Be prepared to ring the changes as much as possible. Spring is just around the corner, so why not get out of the house?

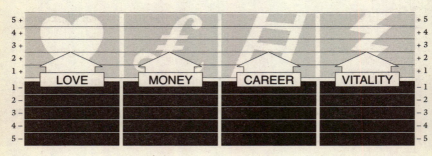

March 2010

YOUR MONTH AT A GLANCE

⊕ = Opportunities are around   ⊖ = Be on the defensive   ◯ = Life is pretty ordinary

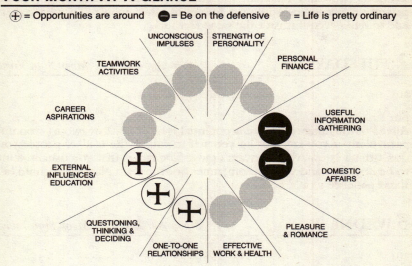

- UNCONSCIOUS IMPULSES
- STRENGTH OF PERSONALITY
- TEAMWORK ACTIVITIES
- PERSONAL FINANCE
- CAREER ASPIRATIONS
- USEFUL INFORMATION GATHERING
- EXTERNAL INFLUENCES/ EDUCATION
- DOMESTIC AFFAIRS
- QUESTIONING, THINKING & DECIDING
- PLEASURE & ROMANCE
- ONE-TO-ONE RELATIONSHIPS
- EFFECTIVE WORK & HEALTH

MARCH HIGHS AND LOWS

Here I show you how the rhythms of the Moon will affect you this month. Like the tide, your energies and abilities will rise and fall with its pattern. When it is above the centre line, go for it, when it is below, you should be resting.

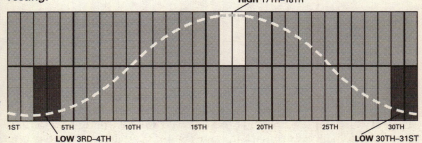

HIGH 17TH–18TH

1ST   5TH   10TH   15TH   20TH   25TH   30TH

LOW 3RD–4TH

LOW 30TH–31ST

1 MONDAY

Moon Age Day 15   Moon Sign Virgo

am ....

pm ....
Whatever you do today, it is likely that you want to be out in front and winning. This may not always be possible, and some frustration could follow if you can't maintain the course you want to take. Try to be patient, especially regarding the foibles of other people. They have their tale to tell – even if it isn't the same as yours.

2 TUESDAY

Moon Age Day 16   Moon Sign Virgo

am ....

pm ....
Ahead of the lunar low there is potential for a conflict or two to crop up, particularly if you can't bring yourself to follow the lead of people you don't think know what they are doing. The fact is that you usually want to be in charge and you are sometimes not the team player you could be. Extra patience would be wise.

3 WEDNESDAY

Moon Age Day 17   Moon Sign Libra

am ....

pm ....
Beware a tendency to be erratic and a desire to do everything all at once. Getting to grips with almost anything can be difficult whilst the lunar low is around, so don't be afraid to sit back and relax for a while. This may not be easy for you, but if you knock your head against a brick wall today you will probably end up with a headache!

4 THURSDAY

Moon Age Day 18   Moon Sign Libra

am ....

pm ....
It might not be too easy for you to feel very motivated today, especially if it appears that everything you undertake is twice as difficult as usual. The advice is simple – don't get too involved and be willing to relax until planetary influences turn back in your favour. Casual conversations offer you scope to find unexpected joy.

5 FRIDAY
Moon Age Day 19   Moon Sign Scorpio

am . . . .

pm . . . .
This is an ideal day to address any intimate issues that require your attention, and since you remain in an essentially reflective frame of mind you will have the time and the patience to look closely at relationships. At home you could discover that comfort and security are more important than usual, and there is much to be said for cuddles.

6 SATURDAY
Moon Age Day 20   Moon Sign Scorpio

am . . . .

pm . . . .
Today's trends assist you to appreciate the difficulties of other people, and you can afford to do all you can to lend a hand. The Sun remains for the moment in your solar twelfth house, an influence that enhances the sensitive side of your nature. Don't be too busy today, and allow for some rest.

7 SUNDAY
Moon Age Day 21   Moon Sign Sagittarius

am . . . .

pm . . . .
It might be slightly difficult to define exactly what you want to do at the present time. Even if you are spoiled for choice, you might also be slightly lethargic when it comes to getting yourself into gear. Rather than worrying about such trends, it's worth spending some time looking around and planning for the medium-term future.

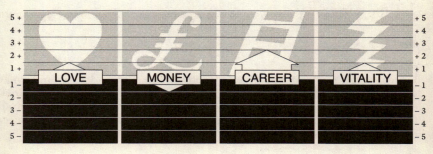

8 MONDAY
Moon Age Day 22   Moon Sign Sagittarius

am . . . .

pm . . . .
You would be wise to reserve some time today for meditation. Your mind is often running ahead of itself, but things sometimes go better for you when you take a short break and simply contemplate nothing in particular. A little prior planning would also be advantageous whilst the Sun remains in your solar twelfth house.

9 TUESDAY
Moon Age Day 23   Moon Sign Capricorn

am . . . .

pm . . . .
The position of the Moon today could be fortunate in helping you to give that last little push to something you have seen as being quite important of late. You can still exhibit your usual drive and determination, even if these are somewhat overpowered by all those twelfth-house planets at the moment. The real effort comes later.

10 WEDNESDAY
Moon Age Day 24   Moon Sign Capricorn

am . . . .

pm . . . .
If ever there was a period for Aries to achieve a high degree of self-discovery, that time is at hand. You have scope to look deep inside yourself, and you don't have to be quite as communicative as would normally be the case. This doesn't mean you have to be moody, and you can still make sure you are very easy to get along with.

11 THURSDAY
Moon Age Day 25   Moon Sign Capricorn

am . . . .

pm . . . .
From a social point of view this has potential be a busy day. Even if you wish to withdraw from the mainstream of life, it is possible that people or circumstances won't allow you to do so. A wider circle of friends is forecast for later in the month, and there is much to be said for starting the ball rolling now.

12 FRIDAY

Moon Age Day 26   Moon Sign Aquarius

am . . . .

pm . . . .
The romantic side of Aries is emphasised today, and you could also be in the market for meeting new and dynamic individuals. With everything to play for at work you have everything you need to finish the working week with a flourish, but that really depends on whether you can be bothered to make a truly significant effort.

13 SATURDAY

Moon Age Day 27   Moon Sign Aquarius

am . . . .

pm . . . .
Logic and concentration may be difficult to find this weekend, which is why you might be better off doing things that don't really take that much thinking about. Routines shouldn't bother you in the slightest, even those that have a domestic slant. In the main, you will probably be happiest today in the bosom of your family.

14 SUNDAY

Moon Age Day 28   Moon Sign Pisces

am . . . .

pm . . . .
With the Moon now also in your solar twelfth house you could still be looking for peace and privacy. If you work at the weekend, you may well find progress in that direction to be slowed to snail's pace. The time is nearly right for you to inject a little more excitement into your life, so be prepared to act in the days ahead.

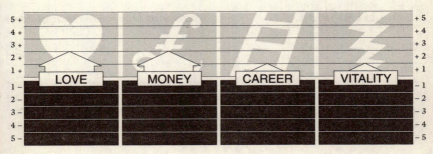

15 MONDAY

Moon Age Day 0   Moon Sign Pisces

am . . . .

pm . . . .
It might seem as though life is passing you by and as if friends and colleagues are sidelining you in some way. Everyone has to go through quieter phases in their life, but the process is more awkward for Aries than any other zodiac sign. On the one hand you need to contemplate, but on the other you feel somehow left out.

16 TUESDAY

Moon Age Day 1   Moon Sign Pisces

am . . . .

pm . . . .
In another day or so you have a chance to change everything for the better. This is not to infer that anything is going wrong just now – it's simply that contentment may be difficult when there are so many twelfth-house influences in your solar chart. Clear the decks for action, because there are far more rewarding and comfortable times to come.

17 WEDNESDAY

Moon Age Day 2   Moon Sign Aries

am . . . .

pm . . . .
The lunar high is a time to make your own luck. Although you may still be slightly held back by your present need to think about everything deeply, you also have what it takes to put in that extra bit of effort that can make all the difference. At work you can really show your potential and enthuse those around you with your bursts of energy.

18 THURSDAY

Moon Age Day 3   Moon Sign Aries

am . . . .

pm . . . .
A day to put your strengths to good use and ignore those parts of your nature with which you are not satisfied. You should now be able to achieve a noticeable improvement in general progress and to turn your mind to matters that have been waiting for a while. The focus is on organisation and diversification.

19 FRIDAY

Moon Age Day 4   Moon Sign Taurus

am . . . .

pm . . . .
When it comes to getting the most from professional matters you needn't be held back at this stage of the week. It's time to show colleagues what you can do and to offer help and advice when they need it. It isn't hard for you to do whatever is necessary, and yet still have time to assist those who are less sure.

20 SATURDAY

Moon Age Day 5   Moon Sign Taurus

am . . . .

pm . . . .
Even if you aren't logical or practical at the start of this weekend, listening to that little voice at the back of your mind will help you to decide how to proceed. From a social point of view you should be at your best right now, and can demonstrate how deep your love really is. Don't be surprised if people want to have you around.

21 SUNDAY

Moon Age Day 6   Moon Sign Taurus

am . . . .

pm . . . .
You have the talent to work out what is most important and to concentrate on that. The reason for the subtle alterations that now come over your nature is the changing positions of the Sun, Mercury and Venus, all of which are lining up to offer greater incentives and more energy as March gets older. Make the most of kind offers.

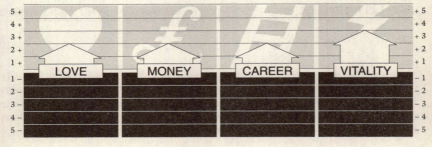

22 MONDAY   *Moon Age Day 7   Moon Sign Gemini*

am . . . .

pm . . . .
Dealing with a variety of different interests should cause you no real difficulty at this time, and there is much to be said for sorting out anything you feel has been waiting around too long. This is not a day to get distracted by trivial matters. It's time to do whatever you can to move plans forward as a new working week gets started.

23 TUESDAY   *Moon Age Day 8   Moon Sign Gemini*

am . . . .

pm . . . .
The Moon moves into your solar fourth house, encouraging you to direct your gaze back towards home and family. Ask yourself whether there is anything you can do to make your partner or close family members feel happier and more secure. It should only take a little effort on your part to make someone feel really good.

24 WEDNESDAY   *Moon Age Day 9   Moon Sign Cancer*

am . . . .

pm . . . .
Venus is now in your solar first house, a precursor of the changes that are going to be possible in your life in the days ahead. You can afford to be courteous, good to know and far less demanding than can sometimes be the case. The keyword here is co-operation, and your strength lies in your ability to become a team player.

25 THURSDAY   *Moon Age Day 10   Moon Sign Cancer*

am . . . .

pm . . . .
Now the Sun has also moved, and its new first-house position offers all the incentives you need to show yourself at your Aries best. What is most appealing about you right now is your ability to instil faith in others. Not only can you convince them that you are bound to succeed, you can also encourage more confidence in themselves.

26 FRIDAY

Moon Age Day 11   Moon Sign Leo

am . . . .

pm . . . .
Where communication issues are concerned, you should now be at your best. Trends stimulate plenty of vitality and a great desire to do as many different jobs as possible. Even if you create plenty of excitement now, you would be wise to be just a little careful that you are not taking on more than anyone – even you – could manage.

27 SATURDAY

Moon Age Day 12   Moon Sign Leo

am . . . .

pm . . . .
In any situation you now benefit from paying attention. Things have potential to go wrong if you take your eye off the ball. It is likely that you are competitive, anxious to win and quite willing to go that extra step in order to achieve your objectives. If others aren't quite so dynamic, you will have to work hard to take them with you.

28 SUNDAY

Moon Age Day 13   Moon Sign Virgo

am . . . .

pm . . . .
Deep inside yourself you can remain calm and assured that the path you are taking through life is the correct one. You can make today an island of peace in an otherwise extremely busy life and should take some time out to watch the flowers grow. A day to spend time with your partner, family members or friends, and to be content.

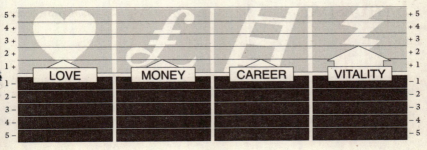

29 MONDAY
Moon Age Day 14   Moon Sign Virgo

am . . . .

pm . . . .
Don't be afraid to welcome someone you haven't seen for quite some time back into your life now, maybe at work or in some way associated with your social life. This could encourage you to be fairly nostalgic, something that doesn't happen very often to Aries. In a practical sense you know how to get things moving successfully.

30 TUESDAY
Moon Age Day 15   Moon Sign Libra

am . . . .

pm . . . .
The lunar low arrives, and it could seem as though the brakes are being applied, especially when it comes to work or tasks that require a good deal of energy. It might be best to leave something until later, otherwise it may end up being done with less panache than usual. Catching up on communications would be no bad thing.

31 WEDNESDAY
Moon Age Day 16   Moon Sign Libra

am . . . .

pm . . . .
Some advancement remains possible, and all those first-house planets tend to overpower the lunar low this month. There is much to be said for thinking deeply to gain a good sense of what works well for you. On those occasions when others disagree with your intentions, it's worth talking them round as only you can.

1 THURSDAY
Moon Age Day 17   Moon Sign Scorpio

am . . . .

pm . . . .
You now have exactly what it takes to put your deepest feelings into words, and in the process to make a positive impression on those around you. Nowhere is this more obvious than in terms of your love life. Emotions become easy to express and you should be able to put your thoughts across in a very poetical way.

2 FRIDAY
Moon Age Day 18   Moon Sign Scorpio

am . . . .

pm . . . .
When it comes to general accomplishments you show yourself to be capable and determined. Don't allow yourself to become bogged down with pointless rules and regulations, because you are probably better when you can please yourself. This might mean taking a few shortcuts, but you can persuade colleagues and friends to support you.

3 SATURDAY
Moon Age Day 19   Moon Sign Sagittarius

am . . . .

pm . . . .
Mars is far from your solar first house, and in a position that might lead you to overestimate your own abilities on occasion. This would be a pity, because in most respects you should have things running quite smoothly at the moment. If you are overtaken by any particular desire you need to analyse the situation carefully.

4 SUNDAY
Moon Age Day 20   Moon Sign Sagittarius

am . . . .

pm . . . .
Right now the time seems right to expand your spiritual horizons. There is a deep side to the Aries nature, even though it is sometimes swamped by all that practicality. On this particular Sunday you can take time out to look deep inside yourself and to lay down plans for actions that will feed your inner self and not simply make you money.

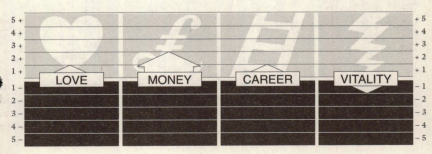

71

April
2010

YOUR MONTH AT A GLANCE

⊕ = Opportunities are around ⊖ = Be on the defensive ⬤ = Life is pretty ordinary

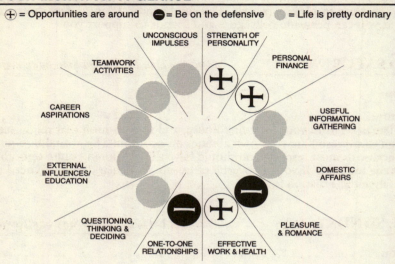

UNCONSCIOUS IMPULSES

STRENGTH OF PERSONALITY

TEAMWORK ACTIVITIES

PERSONAL FINANCE

CAREER ASPIRATIONS

USEFUL INFORMATION GATHERING

EXTERNAL INFLUENCES/ EDUCATION

DOMESTIC AFFAIRS

QUESTIONING, THINKING & DECIDING

PLEASURE & ROMANCE

ONE-TO-ONE RELATIONSHIPS

EFFECTIVE WORK & HEALTH

APRIL HIGHS AND LOWS

Here I show you how the rhythms of the Moon will affect you this month. Like the tide, your energies and abilities will rise and fall with its pattern. When it is above the centre line, go for it, when it is below, you should be resting.

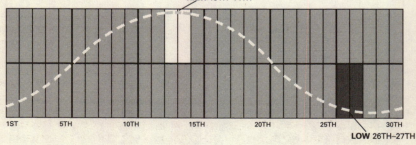

HIGH 13TH–14TH

1ST 5TH 10TH 15TH 20TH 25TH 30TH

LOW 26TH–27TH

5 MONDAY   *Moon Age Day 21   Moon Sign Sagittarius*

am . . . .

pm . . . .
Personal security will probably mean a great deal to you at the moment.
At the same time you are strongly motivated to enjoy the sensual side of
life, and you would be wise to be careful that you don't overindulge!
There will be some luck available as far as financial matters are concerned,
though even here a little caution is necessary.

6 TUESDAY   *Moon Age Day 22   Moon Sign Capricorn*

am . . . .

pm . . . .
Present trends encourage you to display a larger-than-life image, and with
all those first-house planetary positions you can fire on all cylinders and
achieve something practically all of the time. There might be little or no
time for routines if you decide to break the mould in everything you do.
Others might have difficulty keeping up.

7 WEDNESDAY   *Moon Age Day 23   Moon Sign Capricorn*

am . . . .

pm . . . .
Mercury has already moved on into your solar second house and this
could be an important planetary position as far as money is concerned. It
supports a more careful approach in which you should be looking at the
bigger picture in terms of career prospects. An ideal time to glean
interesting details from people at work.

8 THURSDAY   *Moon Age Day 24   Moon Sign Aquarius*

am . . . .

pm . . . .
Even if you continue to be fond of the good life, it's worth focusing your
effort at the moment on work and practical matters. This might mean
trying to burn the candle at both ends, which invariably results in fatigue.
Even Aries cannot keep going for ever without a break, so be prepared to
find something relaxing to do in your down time.

9 FRIDAY
Moon Age Day 25   Moon Sign Aquarius

am . . . .

pm . . . .
You remain lightning-fast when making up your mind and should continue to be so whilst the Sun is in its present position. Others may watch and wait, but ploughing on regardless is your favoured approach. You might appear to some to be reckless, unless you make it quite obvious that you know exactly what you are doing.

10 SATURDAY
Moon Age Day 26   Moon Sign Aquarius

am . . . .

pm . . . .
Although you may be quite transparent in a work or practical sense, emotions might be a different matter. The present position of the Moon promotes a more secretive interlude in which you may be inclined to hide your true feelings. Even if you are very busy, there is much to be said for finding time to explain yourself fully to others.

11 SUNDAY
Moon Age Day 27   Moon Sign Pisces

am . . . .

pm . . . .
With Venus now entering your solar second house you have an opportunity to boost your finances. This particular influence helps you to prosper and grow, mainly because of the good ideas you have and your present ability to put them into action. Standing up for a friend might also be important during this period.

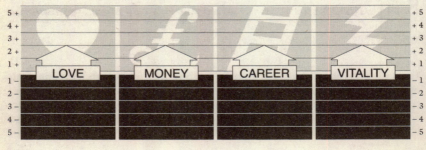

12 MONDAY
Moon Age Day 28   Moon Sign Pisces

am . . . .

pm . . . .
The focus is on enjoying just about any pleasure that comes your way. You can afford to seek the limelight at the start of this week, and it shouldn't bother you in the slightest if people are constantly asking your advice. As is often the case, you know what you want from life and have a very good idea about how to get it.

13 TUESDAY
Moon Age Day 29   Moon Sign Aries

am . . . .

pm . . . .
The luckiest trends of the month get underway, and all you have to do in order to reap the benefits is to be in the best place to take advantage of them. There is no time to be too humble or to deny your capabilities. Give of your best and you will not simply help your own life. On the contrary, you can make sure others benefit too.

14 WEDNESDAY
Moon Age Day 0   Moon Sign Aries

am . . . .

pm . . . .
They say that knowledge is power, and that could certainly be the case as far as you are concerned at this time. Why not take all that confidence and use it in practical ways? You may also decide to cast an eye back to the dim and distant past. Perhaps an idea that you didn't follow up previously is now ripe for development.

15 THURSDAY
Moon Age Day 1   Moon Sign Taurus

am . . . .

pm . . . .
In terms of money, you now enter a phase during which you can make some fairly significant gains. That's why it is important to keep your eyes open and to be willing to move at a moment's notice. Nobody is better at acting on impulse than Aries, but you rarely do so without having at least a strong intuition regarding your actions.

16 FRIDAY

Moon Age Day 2   Moon Sign Taurus

am . . . .

pm . . . .
Rising to daily challenges as and when they appear is the best way to keep on top of things, even if life is inclined to be very busy at present. By all means enjoy feelings of self-satisfaction, but beware of allowing these to get in your way. What matters throughout this time is your view of the next horizon – and then the next.

17 SATURDAY

Moon Age Day 3   Moon Sign Taurus

am . . . .

pm . . . .
Going from one place to another offers you a chance to meet many people today. Staying still is probably not an option when Aries is in this frame of mind, and it is constant stimulation that counts the most. Even if some of your associations with others are fleeting, they needn't be unimportant.

18 SUNDAY ☿

Moon Age Day 4   Moon Sign Gemini

am . . . .

pm . . . .
You have a great ability to attract the finer things of life and this Sunday might give you just a little time to appreciate some of them. It is often the case that material things stand out as being very important, which can make you something of a gadget freak. That's fine, as long as you bear in mind what is really important to you.

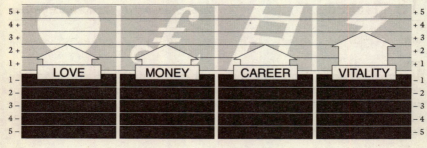

19 MONDAY   ☿   *Moon Age Day 5   Moon Sign Gemini*

am . . . .

pm . . . .
It looks as though you may be tied more firmly to the past in some way
at the start of this working week, and it is the present position of the
Moon that is responsible. This could be particularly true in terms of
personal attachments, which you might be viewing in a rather old-
fashioned way. Keep your mind firmly fixed on now.

20 TUESDAY   ☿   *Moon Age Day 6   Moon Sign Cancer*

am . . . .

pm . . . .
An assertive approach to romantic matters is fine, although it may not be
quite what others are expecting. It's a difficult path to steer, because even
if your lover is happy that you make most of the running, you also need
to reassure them that you are sensitive to their needs and the way they
feel about situations.

21 WEDNESDAY   ☿   *Moon Age Day 7   Moon Sign Cancer*

am . . . .

pm . . . .
This remains a strong period as far as finances are concerned, and
although it would not be sensible to take too many chances you seem to
know instinctively what sort of action you should take. The deeper side
of your nature can be brought more to the fore, but in the main the
trends support an essentially materialistic frame of mind.

22 THURSDAY   ☿   *Moon Age Day 8   Moon Sign Leo*

am . . . .

pm . . . .
Be prepared to get the best from the material world and to sort out any
issues that have been waiting in the wings for a while. There is more in
the way of luxury on offer, but this might only really interest you because
it reflects your success. At heart you are probably happy to get by with
very little ornamentation.

23 FRIDAY ☿ *Moon Age Day 9   Moon Sign Leo*

am . . . .

pm . . . .
There's nothing wrong with thinking about your appearance, especially as the way you look reflects your ability to get things right in your life. How you appear to others is of even greater importance whilst the Moon occupies its present position, and this is particularly significant if you are trying to impress a potential romantic partner.

24 SATURDAY ☿ *Moon Age Day 10   Moon Sign Virgo*

am . . . .

pm . . . .
In a material sense you will now have the ability to loosen a few bonds that have restricted you for a while. A continued reliance on others is not the best way forward, and present planetary trends encourage you to be out on your own to a greater extent. Of course you may still need others, but possibly less so financially speaking.

25 SUNDAY ☿ *Moon Age Day 11   Moon Sign Virgo*

am . . . .

pm . . . .
Your plans for the future appear to be realistic and achievable – at least that is what you can make everyone around you think. The time for taking massive chances is now receding for a while, and it's worth being more careful in the way you assess situations. Affairs of the heart are well starred, so make sure you have time for them.

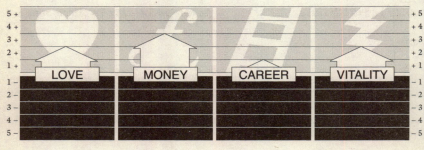

LOVE   MONEY   CAREER   VITALITY

26 MONDAY   ☿   *Moon Age Day 12   Moon Sign Libra*

am . . . .

pm . . . .
You may not be at your best today or tomorrow, and for that you can thank the arrival of the lunar low. You can afford to let others make some of the running and to hold back somewhat when it comes to taking the initiative. We all need thinking time and even Aries needs to rest and reflect occasionally. But will you realise this?

27 TUESDAY   ☿   *Moon Age Day 13   Moon Sign Libra*

am . . . .

pm . . . .
Do you have a strong inner feeling that you must pull yourself together and get on with things more quickly than you seem able to do? Remember that charging forward whilst the lunar low is around is akin to constantly knocking your head against a brick wall. It won't achieve anything, except to give you a totally unnecessary headache!

28 WEDNESDAY   ☿   *Moon Age Day 14   Moon Sign Scorpio*

am . . . .

pm . . . .
The Moon moves on and you once again enter a phase when you have scope to make money and solidify your best-laid plans. What is more, present planetary trends can make financial planning so much easier. At the same time there is much to be said for seeking sound advice from someone who is in the know.

29 THURSDAY   ☿   *Moon Age Day 15   Moon Sign Scorpio*

am . . . .

pm . . . .
Trends encourage you to take responsibility for your own life, which is not at all difficult for the average Aries subject. At the same time there's nothing wrong with showing concern for family members or friends who have been having a difficult time of late. The charitable side of your nature is pricked by almost everything you see.

30 FRIDAY   ☿   *Moon Age Day 16*   *Moon Sign Scorpio*

am . . . .

pm . . . .
Mars remains stubbornly in your solar fifth house, where it has been for ages. Its presence there highlights your passion and could make you slightly less materialistic than would usually be the case when the Sun is in your solar second house. Even if you aren't exactly smouldering at the moment, you can convince others that you are.

1 SATURDAY   ☿   *Moon Age Day 17*   *Moon Sign Sagittarius*

am . . . .

pm . . . .
Now is the time to capitalise on the chance to do something totally off the wall or even slightly outrageous. One option is to join forces with friends to be impressive and brave. Your present state of mind assists you to create a positive impression, and to get at least some of what you want, without having to put in too much effort.

2 SUNDAY   ☿   *Moon Age Day 18*   *Moon Sign Sagittarius*

am . . . .

pm . . . .
You can tap into some fortunate influences now, and should be thinking up new ways to get money and to make the best use of what you already have. There is little doubt about your talent and energy, and this might be a good time to really flex your muscles in some way. An ideal day to stick with friends and find ways to amuse them.

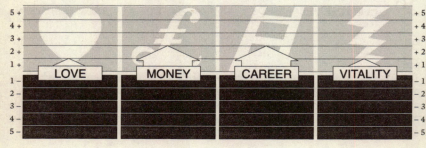

May 2010

YOUR MONTH AT A GLANCE

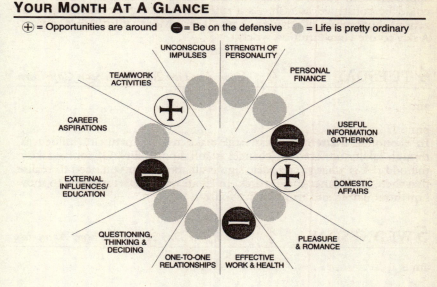

⊕ = Opportunities are around   ⊖ = Be on the defensive   ● = Life is pretty ordinary

UNCONSCIOUS IMPULSES

STRENGTH OF PERSONALITY

TEAMWORK ACTIVITIES

PERSONAL FINANCE

CAREER ASPIRATIONS

USEFUL INFORMATION GATHERING

EXTERNAL INFLUENCES/ EDUCATION

DOMESTIC AFFAIRS

QUESTIONING, THINKING & DECIDING

ONE-TO-ONE RELATIONSHIPS

EFFECTIVE WORK & HEALTH

PLEASURE & ROMANCE

MAY HIGHS AND LOWS

Here I show you how the rhythms of the Moon will affect you this month. Like the tide, your energies and abilities will rise and fall with its pattern. When it is above the centre line, go for it, when it is below, you should be resting.

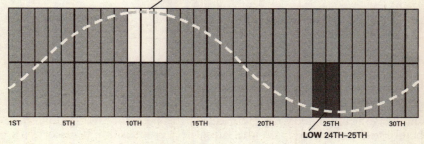

HIGH 10TH–12TH

1ST   5TH   10TH   15TH   20TH   25TH   30TH

LOW 24TH–25TH

3 MONDAY ☿ *Moon Age Day 19* *Moon Sign Capricorn*

am . . . .

pm . . . .
Rather than being overoptimistic at the start of this week, your best approach is to exercise some caution before you take any action that could be construed as rash. As a rule you are very careful about your actions, but beware of relying too much on advice that isn't all it appears. A day to use your intuition wisely.

4 TUESDAY ☿ *Moon Age Day 20* *Moon Sign Capricorn*

am . . . .

pm . . . .
In economic matters you can still make use of fortunate influences, though taking unnecessary chances is still a possibility. Of course taking the odd risk is what your zodiac sign is all about, but you need to realise that there is a balance to be struck. In affairs of the heart it's time to show how honourable and trustworthy you can be.

5 WEDNESDAY ☿ *Moon Age Day 21* *Moon Sign Aquarius*

am . . . .

pm . . . .
You have what it takes at the moment to show yourself at your most elegant and impressive. When you are in social situations you can shine brightly, and can make the most favourable of impressions when it matters the most. Creative potential is well starred at present, though this doesn't mean you can do absolutely anything!

6 THURSDAY ☿ *Moon Age Day 22* *Moon Sign Aquarius*

am . . . .

pm . . . .
Good ideas are to the fore – though there is nothing especially surprising about that for Aries. By all means bring new innovations into your life and once again enjoy your gadget-freak mentality to the full. But before you go out and buy the latest electronic fashion accessory, it's worth asking yourself whether you really need it.

7 FRIDAY
☿ *Moon Age Day 23   Moon Sign Aquarius*

am . . . .

pm . . . .
Subtlety is required today, and that is something you don't always demonstrate to a great degree. If you rush at things you will find difficulties arising, and a light and gentle touch on the tiller of life is the best course under present trends. Ahead of the weekend you have scope to enlarge your social circle in some specific way.

8 SATURDAY
☿ *Moon Age Day 24   Moon Sign Pisces*

am . . . .

pm . . . .
New and unforeseen opportunities are present throughout most of the weekend, but you won't find any of them if you stick too close to home. As the weather improves so you need to spread your wings and to get out into the big, wide world. Even if you are tired by the time the weekend comes, you can afford to ring the changes.

9 SUNDAY
☿ *Moon Age Day 25   Moon Sign Pisces*

am . . . .

pm . . . .
Your potential good fortune in the financial sphere of life is boosted no end by the present position of the Sun in your solar second house. It allows you to be perceptive and open to suggestion, but at the same time encourages a careful approach with your assets. Be prepared to offer advice today if this is requested.

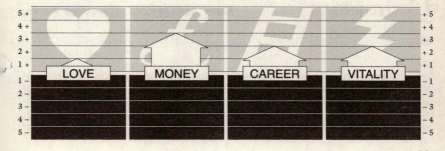

10 MONDAY ☿ *Moon Age Day 26   Moon Sign Aries*

am . . . .

pm . . . .
Your unquenchable desire for change is at its peak now and the lunar high is the ideal time to break new ground. There are some interesting situations in store, and the chance to ensure that your efforts from the past now bring significant rewards. If there is a problem at all, it could be that you are rushing.

11 TUESDAY ☿ *Moon Age Day 27   Moon Sign Aries*

am . . . .

pm . . . .
Any tendency to restrict the possibilities of your life can be put to one side whilst the Moon is in your own zodiac sign of Aries. Vitality is the order of the day, and you are in a position to give a boost to the efforts of family members, as well as colleagues. By giving others a leg up you might also be able to help yourself.

12 WEDNESDAY ☿ *Moon Age Day 28   Moon Sign Aries*

am . . . .

pm . . . .
This is a day of potential financial gains, though you will need to put in an extra bit of effort yourself if you are going to wring the most out of the fading lunar high later in the day. The position of Mercury in your solar chart helps you to keep focused and to speak up for what you want. It's worth seeking support from colleagues.

13 THURSDAY *Moon Age Day 29   Moon Sign Taurus*

am . . . .

pm . . . .
It is towards material goals that you are still inclined to turn. There is an opportunity to display your organisational skills at the present time, and you shouldn't have any difficulty in getting others to do your bidding. When it comes to affairs of the heart, there's nothing wrong with a slightly coy attitude for now.

14 FRIDAY

Moon Age Day 0   Moon Sign Taurus

am . . . .

pm . . . .
Your relationships and encounters with others are well accented, and you can definitely gain from situations in which you co-operate rather than compete. Be prepared to seek out some good news now or across the weekend, even if it turns out that you doubt what you hear at first.

15 SATURDAY

Moon Age Day 1   Moon Sign Gemini

am . . . .

pm . . . .
There isn't much doubt that at the moment trends encourage you to be responsive to variety and change. This isn't at all unusual for the sign of Aries, but the tendency is very marked at present. You can make full use of your ability to concentrate whilst so many planets occupy your solar second house, and you shouldn't easily be duped.

16 SUNDAY

Moon Age Day 2   Moon Sign Gemini

am . . . .

pm . . . .
All you really need to make the planetary line-up complete for the second part of this weekend is something that assists you in fun and leisure. This comes from the direction of the planet Mars, which is still in your solar fifth house. An ideal day to make alterations in or around your home, and to make use of any good weather.

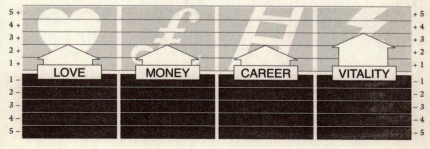

17 MONDAY

Moon Age Day 3   Moon Sign Cancer

am . . . .

pm . . . .
You can now tap into an almost uncanny sense for the moods of people with whom you come into contact. This isn't a long-lived trend because it is responsive to the Moon, but it does assist you today and tomorrow to be super-sensitive to loved ones, friends and colleagues. Don't be afraid to back your hunches at this time.

18 TUESDAY

Moon Age Day 4   Moon Sign Cancer

am . . . .

pm . . . .
The second-house influences begin to break up slightly as Venus moves on into your third solar house. This promotes a more restless nature, though it can also encourage you to be more communicative when it comes to expressing your emotions. Bear in mind that there is more to life than material gain, and that love counts the most.

19 WEDNESDAY

Moon Age Day 5   Moon Sign Leo

am . . . .

pm . . . .
Trends suggest that you may be channelling a lot of energy into a number of different pursuits at the present time. Ask yourself whether you would get on better if you concentrated more in one particular direction. A lack of focus could lead to moderate results, and that may not be good enough for the average Aries subject.

20 THURSDAY

Moon Age Day 6   Moon Sign Leo

am . . . .

pm . . . .
There is a generous and warm side to your nature that helps you to be popular with others and allows you to get much of what you want simply by using persuasion. Using this skill is far better than being at odds with anyone. Competition can only take you so far under present trends, and co-operation is likely to work far better.

21 FRIDAY

Moon Age Day 7   Moon Sign Virgo

am . . . .

pm . . . .
Venus is speeding through the zodiac at the moment and is now resident in your solar fourth house. This encourages you to concentrate on domestic circumstances and family relationships. Now is the time to look carefully at something those close to you have been asking for. It's also worth listening more closely to what they have to say.

22 SATURDAY

Moon Age Day 8   Moon Sign Virgo

am . . . .

pm . . . .
The Sun is also on the move and now occupies your solar third house, where it will remain for the next month or so. This should enhance your powers of communication and offer you the chance to really get to grips with people who haven't been so easy to approach in the past. You should also be willing to go against convention.

23 SUNDAY

Moon Age Day 9   Moon Sign Virgo

am . . . .

pm . . . .
As today wears on it might seem as though you are gradually running out of steam. This is the approach of the lunar low and it could easily take the wind out of your sails for the next couple of days. You can afford to take advantage of Sunday by having a good rest. Make the most of conversations with family members.

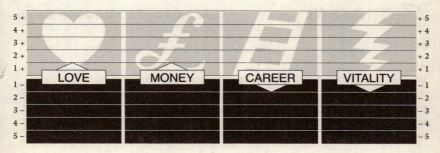

24 MONDAY
Moon Age Day 10   Moon Sign Libra

am . . . .

pm . . . .
This has potential to be a rather sluggish period in which you may not be able to get to grips with matters in the way you normally would. You needn't get too upset about this, because on the plus side you have a chance to think deeply and to work out all manner of complications in your life that are normally very difficult to address.

25 TUESDAY
Moon Age Day 11   Moon Sign Libra

am . . . .

pm . . . .
Even if you are still not on top form, as the day advances there is scope for you to push your ideas through. An ideal day to make travel arrangements for later in the year and to listen to what others have to say about possible destinations. You may even benefit from planning to go somewhere totally different.

26 WEDNESDAY
Moon Age Day 12   Moon Sign Scorpio

am . . . .

pm . . . .
Now it is possible to put every idea to good use. You are generally so sure of yourself that you can get those around you to follow your lead at every turn. Beware of getting involved in family arguments or disputes with friends that are not even worth the effort. Ignore anything that distracts you from the direction you want to follow.

27 THURSDAY
Moon Age Day 13   Moon Sign Scorpio

am . . . .

pm . . . .
Monetary opportunities are clearly in the offing at this time, assisting you to find ways to make cash go much further. Your responsiveness to romantic overtures is highlighted, and Aries subjects who are between relationships at the moment can use this interlude to look for that someone special. Keep up with innovations now.

28 FRIDAY
Moon Age Day 14   Moon Sign Sagittarius

am . . . .

pm . . . .
The Sun in the third house helps you to attract the interest of others, even though you might not personally feel any different. This would be a fine time to try out some new plans for the future, and you have all the incentives you need to push forward on the romantic front. You have what it takes to get people to understand you instinctively.

29 SATURDAY
Moon Age Day 15   Moon Sign Sagittarius

am . . . .

pm . . . .
A potentially restless interlude when you may decide you want to break from your usual routines. This trend has actually been around for a while and is responsive to that fifth-house Mars, which doesn't seem to be moving at all. The upside is that you can deal with any situations that are stagnating and go that extra mile to force issues.

30 SUNDAY
Moon Age Day 16   Moon Sign Capricorn

am . . . .

pm . . . .
In a professional sense the trends are getting better and better. This may play no part in your life today unless you work at the weekend, but it will allow you to lay down plans you can put into action in the days ahead. Your strength lies in your ability to see your path very clearly and to gather the allies you will need for a new push.

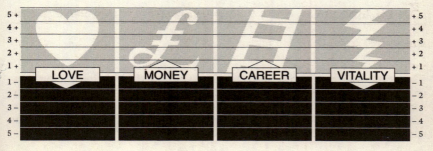

31 MONDAY
Moon Age Day 17   Moon Sign Capricorn

am . . . .

pm . . . .
Relationships with others can now be strengthened because Venus becomes more secure in your fourth house of home and family. Even if you are giving more of your attention to sorting out family issues, at the same time there may be demands being made of you out there in the wider world. Some balance is called for.

1 TUESDAY
Moon Age Day 18   Moon Sign Capricorn

am . . . .

pm . . . .
Along comes June, and you are in a position to begin the first of the true summer months with a great deal of enthusiasm and a great sense of humour. If you make sure you are good to have around, people are more likely to seek out your opinions. It's worth trying to get out of doors as much as possible this week.

2 WEDNESDAY
Moon Age Day 19   Moon Sign Aquarius

am . . . .

pm . . . .
The focus is now on short-term plans and financial schemes of one sort or another. You can use your fertile mind to the full, and may even decide to use something from the past to revitalise present ideas. One thing is certain – you shouldn't be short of imagination and can easily alter circumstances to suit your needs.

3 THURSDAY
Moon Age Day 20   Moon Sign Aquarius

am . . . .

pm . . . .
Domestic and family ties are once again under the spotlight. You may even be going through a distinctly nostalgic phase, which though fairly unusual for Aries can be useful in its own way. The one thing you cannot do is to live in the past, and there is much to be said for remaining, as always, a creature of the moment.

4 FRIDAY
Moon Age Day 21   Moon Sign Pisces

am . . . .

pm . . . .
Today can be a freewheeling time that offers opportunities for change and diversity that are vital to your mental health. This may mean fewer chances to stop and watch nature bursting into life. This is a shame because you sometimes miss those very things that are actually more important than any sort of success.

5 SATURDAY
Moon Age Day 22   Moon Sign Pisces

am . . . .

pm . . . .
Being at the forefront of social matters should prove to be interesting this weekend, and if your time is your own you could do worse than to take an outing with your partner or maybe a close friend. There is great depth to your nature, and under present planetary trends you are in a position to show the fact more and more.

6 SUNDAY
Moon Age Day 23   Moon Sign Pisces

am . . . .

pm . . . .
You can make this a very comfortable sort of Sunday, though as the day passes there may be slightly more restlessness and an urge to turn your mind towards practical matters. What you are registering is the arrival of the lunar high, which is likely to be particularly potent this month. Plan now for tomorrow.

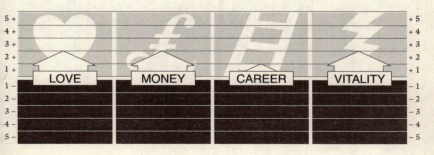

June 2010

YOUR MONTH AT A GLANCE

⊕ = Opportunities are around ⊖ = Be on the defensive ● = Life is pretty ordinary

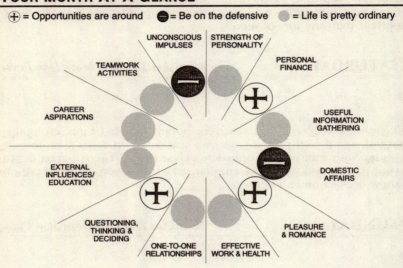

UNCONSCIOUS IMPULSES

STRENGTH OF PERSONALITY

TEAMWORK ACTIVITIES

PERSONAL FINANCE

CAREER ASPIRATIONS

USEFUL INFORMATION GATHERING

EXTERNAL INFLUENCES/ EDUCATION

DOMESTIC AFFAIRS

QUESTIONING, THINKING & DECIDING

ONE-TO-ONE RELATIONSHIPS

EFFECTIVE WORK & HEALTH

PLEASURE & ROMANCE

JUNE HIGHS AND LOWS

Here I show you how the rhythms of the Moon will affect you this month. Like the tide, your energies and abilities will rise and fall with its pattern. When it is above the centre line, go for it, when it is below, you should be resting.

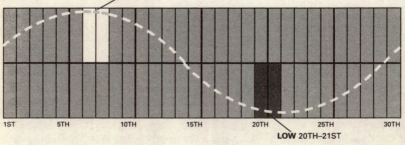

HIGH 7TH–8TH

LOW 20TH–21ST

1ST   5TH   10TH   15TH   20TH   25TH   30TH

7 MONDAY

Moon Age Day 24   Moon Sign Aries

am . . . .

pm . . . .

This would be an extremely good time to trust your intuition and to put that extra bit of effort into tasks you may have been avoiding for a while. With the lunar high around you can make full use of all your energy and determination, and a resolve that cannot be bettered by anyone. Failure is not a concept you understand at present!

8 TUESDAY

Moon Age Day 25   Moon Sign Aries

am . . . .

pm . . . .

You can afford to exhibit a great deal of confidence in your own abilities. This is true for much of the time, but whilst the Moon is in your zodiac sign this tendency is emphasised significantly. Rather than crowding your schedule with routine matters, why not concentrate on areas of your life in which the greatest progress beckons?

9 WEDNESDAY

Moon Age Day 26   Moon Sign Taurus

am . . . .

pm . . . .

Much of what you are doing at the moment can be used to make life easier for you in the future. Casting your mind ahead, it's time to evolve new strategies and work out new ways of solving problems that are going to be of supreme benefit eventually. Long-term thinking isn't always your strategy, but it should work well now.

10 THURSDAY

Moon Age Day 27   Moon Sign Taurus

am . . . .

pm . . . .

Getting together with others can prove to be great fun under present planetary trends, and you have a chance to become extremely popular at the moment. This is not particularly surprising, especially if you show concern for others, make sure you are interesting company and, most important of all, make people laugh!

11 FRIDAY
Moon Age Day 28   Moon Sign Gemini

am . . . .

pm . . . .
Doing just about anything in the company of family and friends has potential to be both interesting and emotionally rewarding today and across the weekend. In a way it doesn't matter who you mix with because you have what it takes to adapt your nature to suit all situations and people. Beware of leaving any important tasks undone today.

12 SATURDAY
Moon Age Day 0   Moon Sign Gemini

am . . . .

pm . . . .
The Sun remains in your solar third house, and this can be a real tonic to Aries because there are times you take yourself too seriously. This position of the Sun assists you to lighten up a good deal and to bring out the humorous and even silly side of your nature. No wonder you can be flavour of the month when in company.

13 SUNDAY
Moon Age Day 1   Moon Sign Gemini

am . . . .

pm . . . .
You have what it takes to be extremely communicative at the moment, and should be willing to join in even casual conversations. Even if not everything seems to have a tangible purpose at the moment, that shouldn't bother you, though you may decide to stay away from people and situations you think are really silly.

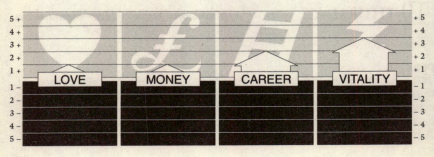

14 MONDAY · Moon Age Day 2 · Moon Sign Cancer

am . . . .

pm . . . .
You needn't be in too much of a hurry with practical tasks today. At the same time it's good to finish one important job before you take on another. If you crowd your schedule too much you could end up discovering that nothing gets done particularly well. That would be a shame when you have scope to be so capable at present.

15 TUESDAY · Moon Age Day 3 · Moon Sign Cancer

am . . . .

pm . . . .
A sense of harmony and ease can be established within your daily routine, and it's all thanks to the planet Venus, which is now occupying your solar fifth house. The focus is on making relationships with loved ones, and indeed with the world at large, placid and happy, even if there is the odd person who tries to annoy you.

16 WEDNESDAY · Moon Age Day 4 · Moon Sign Leo

am . . . .

pm . . . .
Trends indicate a time of movement, and slight difficulties and delays are a distinct possibility when it comes to travel. Your best approach is to try to streamline your plans and make sure that you know before you depart exactly what you intend to do – and when. Being organised at the start avoids some major frustrations later.

17 THURSDAY · Moon Age Day 5 · Moon Sign Leo

am . . . .

pm . . . .
The help of friends could be especially important to you at this stage of the month. Maybe there is someone who is good at a job you hate, or it could be that you need the assistance of a definite expert. The fact is that even though you are an Aries subject, you can't do everything yourself. A little humility would help today.

18 FRIDAY

Moon Age Day 6   Moon Sign Virgo

am . . . .

pm . . . .
Little Mercury now brings you to a mental peak and offers you silver-tongued eloquence. You might even decide to be poetical under the influence of this planet, and could easily find the right words to say 'I love you' to that very special person. There doesn't have to be a birthday or an anniversary – say it anyway!

19 SATURDAY

Moon Age Day 7   Moon Sign Virgo

am . . . .

pm . . . .
This can be a slightly frustrating time, especially if you happen to work at the weekend. The Moon is moving on towards Libra, which it will occupy later in the day. The result is the lunar low, and although it doesn't have the power to depress you or to bring real problems into your life, a rather sluggish interlude is possible.

20 SUNDAY

Moon Age Day 8   Moon Sign Libra

am . . . .

pm . . . .
You would be wise to proceed with caution today and avoid taking on too much at all. If the weather is good, there's nothing wrong with sitting in the garden, or going somewhere really beautiful to simply enjoy the view. If you don't pit yourself against the world whilst the lunar low is around, you may even fail to notice its presence.

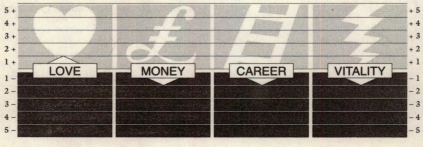

21 MONDAY
Moon Age Day 9   Moon Sign Libra

am . . . .

pm . . . .
These are not the best of trends for a new working week, though once again it has to be said that the position of the Moon only has a profound influence on you at the moment if you allow it to do so. As long as you pace yourself and are willing to take on board the advice and practical help of friends, you can make sure all is well.

22 TUESDAY
Moon Age Day 10   Moon Sign Scorpio

am . . . .

pm . . . .
This would be an excellent time to clear up any unfinished business before you get on with new projects. Be prepared to enlist the support of colleagues at work and friends in social situations. Working with others can give a real boost to your fortunes at this time, particularly if you are willing to adapt your nature to suit different individuals.

23 WEDNESDAY
Moon Age Day 11   Moon Sign Scorpio

am . . . .

pm . . . .
Trends encourage a feeling of self-indulgence at this time, but you need to be careful not to make yourself sluggish or slow in your thinking. It would be better by far to err on the side of caution in terms of what you eat and drink for the next couple of days. Physically speaking, plenty of fresh air and exercise are the order of the day.

24 THURSDAY
Moon Age Day 12   Moon Sign Sagittarius

am . . . .

pm . . . .
Opt for some light relief if possible. Taking yourself or your life too seriously can lead to disappointments, but if you keep your attitude light and airy there is much amusement to be had. Laughter is a real tonic, and one you can also offer to colleagues and friends right now. By the evening you should be acting on impulse.

25 FRIDAY
Moon Age Day 13   Moon Sign Sagittarius

am . . . .

pm . . . .
A nostalgic day is possible with the Sun now in your solar fourth house.
In reality the next three or four weeks might encourage you to look back
much more than would normally be the case. In addition, there is much
to be said for devoting time to thinking about the happiness and
contentment of family members.

26 SATURDAY
Moon Age Day 14   Moon Sign Sagittarius

am . . . .

pm . . . .
If you avoid hurrying things you can achieve a great deal, but putting on
too much of a spurt can result in you tripping over your own feet. Your
best approach is to slow things down a little, since the general pace of
your life is unlikely to be assisted by the present position of Mars, which
has now moved into your solar sixth house.

27 SUNDAY
Moon Age Day 15   Moon Sign Capricorn

am . . . .

pm . . . .
This is an excellent time to re-evaluate career issues, even if you don't
work on a Sunday. There should be time enough for thinking and for
coming to some fairly startling conclusions. What makes this process
possible is your current ability to look at old situations in new and quite
revolutionary ways.

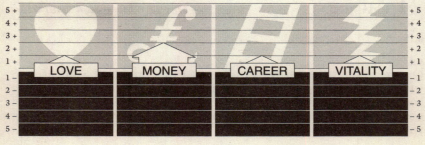

28 MONDAY
Moon Age Day 16   Moon Sign Capricorn

am . . . .

pm . . . .
It looks as though your charisma is at a peak – which might be surprising if you aren't exactly shouting your own abilities to the world at the moment. Slow and steady force applied over a period of time makes far more sense than your usual frenetic bursts of energy. If you demonstrate your potential, others will want to be part of your world.

29 TUESDAY
Moon Age Day 17   Moon Sign Aquarius

am . . . .

pm . . . .
Even if you are caught up in personal issues right now, you can still make today both easy-going and pleasurable. It looks as though Aries can find a new way to present itself and it is one that can certainly be used to impress those around you. Impulsive actions probably don't appeal to you – at least not for the moment.

30 WEDNESDAY
Moon Age Day 18   Moon Sign Aquarius

am . . . .

pm . . . .
By all means remain steady in your approach to life, but it's worth also being ready for a few challenges. Mars pushes you on, as it invariably does, though the position of the Sun continues to offer a more considered approach than usual. This could turn out to be a formidable combination and a source of great interest.

1 THURSDAY
Moon Age Day 19   Moon Sign Aquarius

am . . . .

pm . . . .
Socially and romantically you can be on top form as July gets underway. If there is good weather to be had, be prepared to find fresh fields and pastures new – perhaps even literally. Standard responses to old issues – especially romantic ones – won't necessarily work today, and an alternative strategy could be called for.

2 FRIDAY
Moon Age Day 20   Moon Sign Pisces

am . . . .

pm . . . .
The Moon is now in your solar twelfth house, bringing a concern with personal issues and with secrets you really do want to keep. At the same time little Mercury encourages spilling the beans, so it is obvious that some extra caution is called for. You probably won't be fighting anyone today, except yourself!

3 SATURDAY
Moon Age Day 21   Moon Sign Pisces

am . . . .

pm . . . .
An important relationship, perhaps with an older person, comes under the spotlight around now. There are emotional overtones to your life that are much emphasised by the position of the Moon. By tomorrow everything begins to look quite different, so prepare yourself for a Sunday that could turn out to be sensational.

4 SUNDAY
Moon Age Day 22   Moon Sign Aries

am . . . .

pm . . . .
There is a strong possibility that you can tap into new opportunities whilst the lunar high is around, and you need to be ready to bring all your energy and determination into play. Exactly what you decide to take on remains to be seen, but there isn't much doubt that you can be cool, capable and quite certain of your abilities.

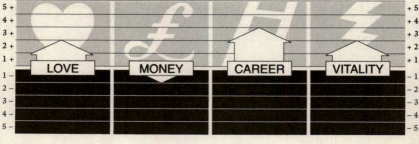

July 2010

YOUR MONTH AT A GLANCE

$\bigoplus$ = Opportunities are around $\bigominus$ = Be on the defensive   ⬤ = Life is pretty ordinary

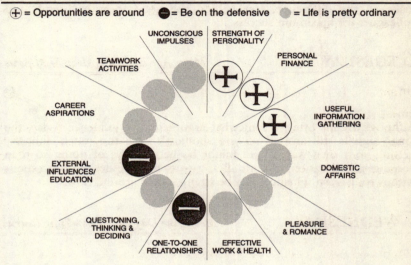

UNCONSCIOUS IMPULSES

STRENGTH OF PERSONALITY

TEAMWORK ACTIVITIES

PERSONAL FINANCE

CAREER ASPIRATIONS

USEFUL INFORMATION GATHERING

EXTERNAL INFLUENCES/ EDUCATION

DOMESTIC AFFAIRS

QUESTIONING, THINKING & DECIDING

ONE-TO-ONE RELATIONSHIPS

EFFECTIVE WORK & HEALTH

PLEASURE & ROMANCE

JULY HIGHS AND LOWS

Here I show you how the rhythms of the Moon will affect you this month. Like the tide, your energies and abilities will rise and fall with its pattern. When it is above the centre line, go for it, when it is below, you should be resting.

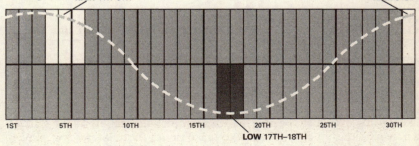

HIGH 4TH–6TH

HIGH 31ST

1ST   5TH   10TH   15TH   20TH   25TH   30TH

LOW 17TH–18TH

5 MONDAY
Moon Age Day 23   Moon Sign Aries

am . . . .

pm . . . .
This is a great period for getting what you want and there could hardly
be a better start to a new week than the lunar high. Whatever you take
on today, be prepared to do it with great confidence, which is what can
make all the difference. Get behind the good ideas of friends and
colleagues for maximum success.

6 TUESDAY
Moon Age Day 24   Moon Sign Aries

am . . . .

pm . . . .
Although trends bring a somewhat argumentative influence today, the
lunar high is still around so you shouldn't have too much difficulty
getting your own way. There might be better ways of doing so than
barging into situations like a bull at a gate, but the desired outcome is
within your grasp. Finances can be strengthened around now.

7 WEDNESDAY
Moon Age Day 25   Moon Sign Taurus

am . . . .

pm . . . .
Getting on top of your finances could well be the number one priority
now, and doing so need present few problems. If there are people around
who are slightly less certain of themselves than you are, some support
shown for them would be useful for all concerned. By the evening you
can afford to turn your mind towards romance.

8 THURSDAY
Moon Age Day 26   Moon Sign Taurus

am . . . .

pm . . . .
This is probably the best time of the month for romance, and the
response you can attract from others in this department of your life is
likely to be extremely positive. Aries subjects who are just at the start of
a new relationship can take steps to make things more interesting, almost
by the moment, particularly if you remain attentive.

9 FRIDAY
Moon Age Day 27   Moon Sign Gemini

am . . . .

pm . . . .
Your family life has potential to be especially rewarding whilst the Sun occupies your solar fourth house, which it does for the next two or three weeks. Devoting time and attention to domestic matters can make a difference now, and this needn't slow you down in a practical sense. An ideal day for bringing situations under control.

10 SATURDAY
Moon Age Day 28   Moon Sign Gemini

am . . . .

pm . . . .
Although this isn't exactly the best time for tackling major ambitions you are still able to push through to your objectives. All the fourth-house associations in your chart encourage a more circumspect approach than usual, and your emotional commitments could well get in the way of your overall desire to succeed materially.

11 SUNDAY
Moon Age Day 29   Moon Sign Cancer

am . . . .

pm . . . .
You can persuade people to be especially helpful today, particularly if you focus on your own attitude. It's worth spending time handing out compliments to family members and especially to your partner. Sometimes you forget just how important a little encouragement can be, and the response you get could be very surprising.

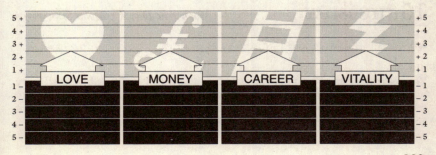

12 MONDAY

Moon Age Day 0   Moon Sign Cancer

am . . . .

pm . . . .
You now have a chance to enjoy the practical world somewhat more than
might have been the case at times last week. Venus has moved on again
in your chart and is now resident in your solar sixth house. At work you
can achieve an easing of the pressure you felt yourself to be under,
especially if you are relaxing more.

13 TUESDAY

Moon Age Day 1   Moon Sign Leo

am . . . .

pm . . . .
The emphasis just now is on the creative side of your nature. Insisting on
having everything around you 'just so' might be fine for you, but maybe
not for the people with whom you live. Getting things done in a practical
sense shouldn't be too difficult today, but will be better still if you co-
operate instead of confront.

14 WEDNESDAY

Moon Age Day 2   Moon Sign Leo

am . . . .

pm . . . .
You have potential to be the quickest-thinking person around at the
present time. This is good as far as career and practical matters are
concerned, and since you are still involved in fourth-house matters it also
helps when it comes to finding the right things to say at home. A day to
please others, who will revel in your kindness.

15 THURSDAY

Moon Age Day 3   Moon Sign Virgo

am . . . .

pm . . . .
Your strong desire to get things done as quickly as possible is all very
well, but it is still important to make sure they are done properly. Any
tendency to rush could well mean having to repeat yourself instead of
achieving your objectives first time. Slow and steady could enable you to
win more than one race today.

16 FRIDAY
Moon Age Day 4   Moon Sign Virgo

am . . . .

pm . . . .
Right now you need to concentrate on the most reliable long-term plans, instead of going for what seems right for the moment. The more effort you put into planning, the greater should be your successes further down the line. In your work it is possible for you to take yourself to the verge of a very important breakthrough.

17 SATURDAY
Moon Age Day 5   Moon Sign Libra

am . . . .

pm . . . .
With a general slow-down in evidence you will have to contend with the lunar low for the next couple of days. If you get yourself into the right frame of mind this needn't be too much of a problem, and it is clear that you have persistence and determination at your command despite the present trends. Why not seek help from friends?

18 SUNDAY
Moon Age Day 6   Moon Sign Libra

am . . . .

pm . . . .
Whatever you decide to do today is best undertaken slowly and without your usual tendency to rush. The fact is that no matter how hard you try, life may well only run at one speed. Once again there is much to be said for relying on the good offices of those around you, and you have the ability to persuade others to lend a helping hand.

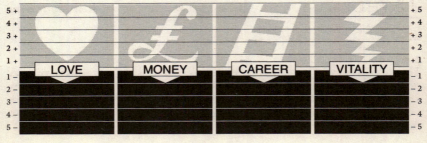

19 MONDAY

Moon Age Day 7   Moon Sign Scorpio

am . . . .

pm . . . .
For the next couple of days the Sun remains in your solar fourth house, putting the spotlight firmly on the domestic scene. Even if it takes you a while to pick yourself up from the more sluggish feel of the lunar low, you can turn this into a really positive week all the same. A favourable time to engage others in stimulating conversations.

20 TUESDAY

Moon Age Day 8   Moon Sign Scorpio

am . . . .

pm . . . .
A few obstacles remain, and most of these are brought about thanks to the present position of Mars in your solar chart. Disputes in the workplace are possible, and your best approach is to be careful what you say to others, for fear of giving offence without wishing to do so. Effectively communicating your ideas might be difficult.

21 WEDNESDAY

Moon Age Day 9   Moon Sign Sagittarius

am . . . .

pm . . . .
Inspiration and energy comes from the direction of Venus, and when it comes to finding the right words to tell people how you feel about them, you can make sure you're at the top of the class. Any remaining small concerns can be dealt with one at a time. In the main you can afford to be feeling quite positive.

22 THURSDAY

Moon Age Day 10   Moon Sign Sagittarius

am . . . .

pm . . . .
The Moon moves on and from its present position it assists you to express yourself more positively. This would be a really good time for new ideas and revised philosophies. It is the sort of period during which you can see how wrong you have been about some ideas, which can set you thinking how to make necessary changes.

23 FRIDAY
Moon Age Day 11   Moon Sign Sagittarius

am . . . .

pm . . . .
Today the Sun moves on into your solar fifth house, bringing a slightly different feel to the next three or four weeks. The time is right to tap into your considerable creative talent, and instead of looking at the purely practical in life it becomes much more important to get things working smoothly. There are financial gains to be made.

24 SATURDAY
Moon Age Day 12   Moon Sign Capricorn

am . . . .

pm . . . .
Do you feel comfortable today with disorder and chaos around you? If you don't, one option is to decide upon a late but necessary spring-clean. This trend does not simply extend to your domestic surroundings because it has much to do with the way your mind is working. Satisfaction can be achieved from sorting things out.

25 SUNDAY
Moon Age Day 13   Moon Sign Capricorn

am . . . .

pm . . . .
The best trends of all today come for those Aries subjects who work at the weekend. Your practical mind can be turned towards getting things running smoothly and you should manage to retain good relationships with co-workers. If you want someone to do your bidding, now is the time to put in some extra effort and to use psychology.

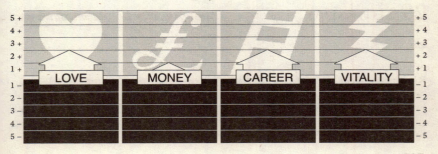

26 MONDAY
Moon Age Day 14   Moon Sign Aquarius

am . . . .

pm . . . .
With the new influence of the fifth-house Sun really beginning to bite it is towards the more creative side of your nature that you are urged to return time and again today. It isn't just important to know that things work in the way they do – you also want to find out why they do. Curiosity becomes the hallmark of your nature at this time.

27 TUESDAY
Moon Age Day 15   Moon Sign Aquarius

am . . . .

pm . . . .
Friendship will prove to be especially important as subtle planetary influences change around you. It is vital for you to know that others love you – much more so than would usually be the case. It looks as though you would happily move mountains in order to know that you are popular, and you show great tenacity in relationships.

28 WEDNESDAY
Moon Age Day 16   Moon Sign Aquarius

am . . . .

pm . . . .
You could well feel your style to be somewhat cramped at the moment, particularly concerning your self-image. As a rule you are more than happy with what you know yourself to be but a little dissatisfaction is possible around now. The middle of this week is not the most comfortable place to be for some Aries subjects.

29 THURSDAY
Moon Age Day 17   Moon Sign Pisces

am . . . .

pm . . . .
Right now you should not be too rash or over keen to get ahead. Your best approach is to watch and wait for a while and make the most of prevailing circumstances rather than trying to alter life too much. You can afford to bring new personalities into your life around this time, and to take on board some of their new ways of thinking.

30 FRIDAY
Moon Age Day 18   Moon Sign Pisces

am . . . .

pm . . . .
Your ability to charm people higher up the career tree than you are is emphasised at the end of this particular week, and you can turn all your attention towards feathering your own nest for later on. Even if there is less of a tendency than usual for you to be impulsive, you can still cause others to sit up and take notice with your actions.

31 SATURDAY
Moon Age Day 19   Moon Sign Aries

am . . . .

pm . . . .
Build your own routines for the weekend and don't be too anxious to do things that simply please those around you. It would be far too easy under present trends to cater for the moment, but that won't stand you in very good stead for the medium and long term. This is a time during which being circumspect is the key.

1 SUNDAY
Moon Age Day 20   Moon Sign Aries

am . . . .

pm . . . .
The lunar high doesn't really begin to show its presence fully until today, but now you can take all the thoughtful moments of yesterday and turn them to your own advantage. If getting on in a career sense isn't an option on a Sunday, why not find ways to inject action and fun into your social life?

YOUR MONTH AT A GLANCE

⊕ = Opportunities are around ⊖ = Be on the defensive ⬤ = Life is pretty ordinary

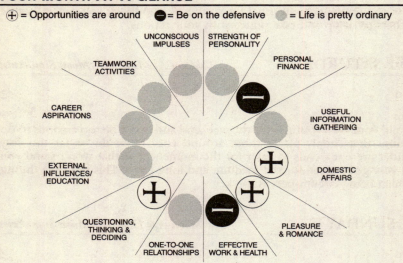

UNCONSCIOUS IMPULSES

STRENGTH OF PERSONALITY

TEAMWORK ACTIVITIES

PERSONAL FINANCE

CAREER ASPIRATIONS

USEFUL INFORMATION GATHERING

EXTERNAL INFLUENCES/ EDUCATION

DOMESTIC AFFAIRS

QUESTIONING, THINKING & DECIDING

PLEASURE & ROMANCE

ONE-TO-ONE RELATIONSHIPS

EFFECTIVE WORK & HEALTH

AUGUST HIGHS AND LOWS

Here I show you how the rhythms of the Moon will affect you this month. Like the tide, your energies and abilities will rise and fall with its pattern. When it is above the centre line, go for it, when it is below, you should be resting. HIGH 1ST–2ND

HIGH 28TH–29TH

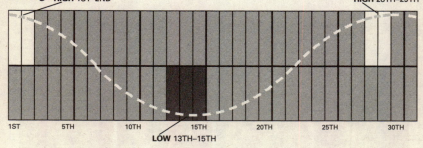

1ST   5TH   10TH   15TH   20TH   25TH   30TH

LOW 13TH–15TH

2 MONDAY

Moon Age Day 21   Moon Sign Aries

am . . . .

pm . . . .
In relationships there could be minor disturbances to be dealt with and a few frustrations that you cannot seem to avoid. Take life steadily and don't try to push issues, because you could so easily annoy others without intending to do so. Someone you haven't seen for a while could be brought back into your life around now.

3 TUESDAY

Moon Age Day 22   Moon Sign Taurus

am . . . .

pm . . . .
You have potential to gain much help and assistance as far as your work is concerned, from both expected and unexpected directions. Be prepared to continue to welcome new personalities into your sphere of influence, and to allow your imagination to be captivated. The only thing missing might be enough time!

4 WEDNESDAY

Moon Age Day 23   Moon Sign Taurus

am . . . .

pm . . . .
You need to express your ideas and opinions freely, and without being thwarted by people who think they know your life better than you do. Try not to get annoyed or overanxious about anyone who interferes, and treat their actions simply as a misdirected concern. In the end you should do what seems right to you.

5 THURSDAY

Moon Age Day 24   Moon Sign Gemini

am . . . .

pm . . . .
Coming up with new ways to get your ideas across to others is what today is about, and your mind is fertile and active. A few potential frustrations do remain, particularly if you can't always get colleagues or friends to do your bidding. Persuasion is the key, because force won't work at all well under present trends.

6 FRIDAY
Moon Age Day 25   Moon Sign Gemini

am . . . .

pm . . . .
When it comes to work and getting things done, you can achieve a great deal by mixing business with pleasure. You can turn colleagues into friends by showing them that you are there for them, even when the working day is over. More practicality is on the way, but it can only be assisted by a good dose of psychology at present.

7 SATURDAY
Moon Age Day 26   Moon Sign Cancer

am . . . .

pm . . . .
You can afford to let major objectives in the outside world take second place to simply enjoying yourself this weekend. It's high summer – an ideal period to find new ways to enjoy what nature is offering all around you. It's time to open your eyes and to take pleasure from the open air, perhaps together with people you really care for.

8 SUNDAY
Moon Age Day 27   Moon Sign Cancer

am . . . .

pm . . . .
At this time you can be an excellent catalyst for getting people together. Be prepared to fascinate others with your zest for life and your sparkling personality. All work and no play can make anyone dull, and this is especially true in the case of Aries. In any case you can turn things that start out as social diversions into practical ideas later on.

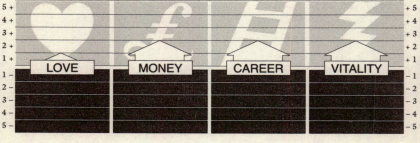

9 MONDAY

Moon Age Day 28   Moon Sign Leo

am . . . .

pm . . . .
Some people might consider you to be slightly self-centred at the moment, and it is true that you do have scope to feather your own nest. However, there will be opportunities to help others get the best out of life too and these should not be ignored today. Don't miss a chance to show people how charitable you can be.

10 TUESDAY

Moon Age Day 0   Moon Sign Leo

am . . . .

pm . . . .
The spotlight is on your radiant personality – with perhaps just a touch of self-importance! There isn't much doubt about your ability to be noticed, and when it comes to taking on new responsibilities in life, this is the time. It is possible that you will be taking yourself just slightly more seriously than is strictly necessary.

11 WEDNESDAY

Moon Age Day 1   Moon Sign Virgo

am . . . .

pm . . . .
Whatever your larger goals in life happen to be, you can analyse them closely under present planetary trends and decide how best to proceed towards your objectives. There is help available if you choose to seek it, but you may decide you would rather plough your own furrow for the moment. Be prepared to offer support to friends.

12 THURSDAY

Moon Age Day 2   Moon Sign Virgo

am . . . .

pm . . . .
There is a lot to learn about compromise at this stage of the week, because you can get on far better if you are willing to share what you know with trusted colleagues and friends. There is also more than one way of looking at specific situations, and you need to realise the fact if you are to get the very best out of what is on offer.

13 FRIDAY

Moon Age Day 3   Moon Sign Libra

am ....

pm ....
Today might seem to be a bit of a drag at times, especially since the lunar low just happens to coincide with Friday the thirteenth this month. Bad luck is not inevitable, but you may have to work extra hard to make any real headway in a practical sense. Why not take a break and allow others to make some of the running?

14 SATURDAY

Moon Age Day 4   Moon Sign Libra

am ....

pm ....
If things don't work out entirely as you wish for the first part of the weekend, one option is to rely on the good offices of your partner or family members in order to get specific tasks done. At this time of year relaxing in the sun is always a possibility and one you might choose to consider today.

15 SUNDAY

Moon Age Day 5   Moon Sign Libra

am ....

pm ....
You may well decide that the end of the lunar low is an ideal time to address some serious matters. A far better approach would be to look to the lighter side of life and to find reasons to laugh as much as possible. Alternative ways of looking at normal situations would also work well whilst you are in this quirky frame of mind.

16 MONDAY
Moon Age Day 6   Moon Sign Scorpio

am . . . .

pm . . . .
You have plenty of surplus energy at your disposal as a new working week gets underway, and you are definitely out of the lunar low period. The Sun remains in your solar fifth house and brings you determination in cart-loads, which is just as well if you have practical decisions to make and many options on offer.

17 TUESDAY
Moon Age Day 7   Moon Sign Scorpio

am . . . .

pm . . . .
Try to stay well away from any tendency to be self-righteous or to adopt an attitude that says 'I am always right'. Bear in mind that others may have a valid point of view and might actually be better informed than you are. By listening to what they have to say, you could avoid causing yourself a few problems further down the line.

18 WEDNESDAY
Moon Age Day 8   Moon Sign Sagittarius

am . . . .

pm . . . .
Look out for potential romance, which is almost certain to be available whilst Venus is in your solar seventh house. Social invitations and chance encounters also have much to offer. This time is all about being amongst other people rather than simply choosing to take your own solitary path through life.

19 THURSDAY
Moon Age Day 9   Moon Sign Sagittarius

am . . . .

pm . . . .
Don't be afraid to be gregarious, talkative and full of beans at the moment in order to attract attention from others. This might be a good time to go for something you have wanted for a while, especially in terms of your career. It's worth thinking about strategies for the autumn months and planning well ahead whilst the going is good.

20 FRIDAY
Moon Age Day 10   Moon Sign Capricorn

am . . . .

pm . . . .
Rather than shying away from crowds under present trends, your best approach is to enjoy the best of what high summer has to offer. There is much to be said for being in the social spotlight and putting yourself forward for special projects. This would be an excellent time to take a trip of some sort.

21 SATURDAY ☿ *Moon Age Day 11   Moon Sign Capricorn*

am . . . .

pm . . . .
You have scope to put your quick brain to good use in all practical matters and to get involved in group activities this weekend. Once again the great outdoors could be calling you, and those Aries subjects who have decided on a holiday right now will be the most fortunate of all. Newer and better ways of expressing yourself are possible.

22 SUNDAY ☿ *Moon Age Day 12   Moon Sign Capricorn*

am . . . .

pm . . . .
This can be a time of happy encounters, and you have everything you need to be making new friends at every turn. Getting others onto your wavelength is one way of gaining the sort of stimulation that you need. Your thought processes are like lightning, and it would take someone very clever to pull the wool over your eyes.

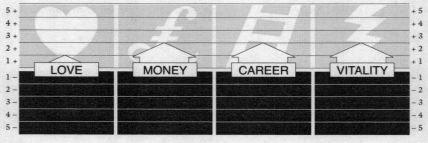

23 MONDAY ☿ *Moon Age Day 13 Moon Sign Aquarius*

am . . . .

pm . . . .
There are signs that not everyone will be equally agreeable today, and you may discover that one particular person is trying to do you a disservice. This is a fairly temporary state of affairs and not one you should react to at all strongly. If things do go slightly wrong, be prepared to simply shrug your shoulders and try again.

24 TUESDAY ☿ *Moon Age Day 14 Moon Sign Aquarius*

am . . . .

pm . . . .
This is an ideal time for practical planning and for sorting out necessary details in your life. The Sun has now entered your solar sixth house and this allows you to look well ahead. It isn't so much today or tomorrow that should be on your mind but rather weeks or months ahead. Make sure others see you as a real personality now.

25 WEDNESDAY ☿ *Moon Age Day 15 Moon Sign Pisces*

am . . . .

pm . . . .
With the Moon in your solar twelfth house a somewhat moody interlude is possible today and tomorrow, but if you stay open to jokes and a light-hearted view of life you have scope to achieve far more. Relatives and friends could be causing some concern and even your life partner might be throwing the odd spanner in the works.

26 THURSDAY ☿ *Moon Age Day 16 Moon Sign Pisces*

am . . . .

pm . . . .
If you don't feel that you are fully in the know today, it's worth seeking a clearer understanding of your partner's feelings. There's nothing wrong with asking a few leading questions and showing that you care. That may be all that is really needed to enable you to nip any specific issues in the bud.

27 FRIDAY
☿   *Moon Age Day 17*   *Moon Sign Pisces*

am . . . .

pm . . . .
New objectives are in view, and as today wears on you should get better and better at scoring significant successes. By the evening it should be evident that the lunar high is having a bearing on your life, particularly if you make use of the energy available. Aries should be fun to have around at all stages of the coming weekend.

28 SATURDAY
☿   *Moon Age Day 18*   *Moon Sign Aries*

am . . . .

pm . . . .
A personal goal can be given the green light now, and there doesn't appear to be any limit to your potential for success. Once you see your objectives you can move towards them quickly, probably ahead of everyone else. Aries is a natural leader and you can show that so clearly now that few people would question the fact.

29 SUNDAY
☿   *Moon Age Day 19*   *Moon Sign Aries*

am . . . .

pm . . . .
Characterised by high energy and a great deal of native wit, the lunar high helps you to push in the direction of your most cherished ambitions. If it proves to be impossible to address significant practical issues on a Sunday, why not turn your attention to having a good time? If you're on form, it's time to be the life and soul of the party!

30 MONDAY ☿ *Moon Age Day 20 Moon Sign Taurus*

am . . . .

pm . . . .
You can still make plenty of interesting things happen as far as your social life is concerned, and take advantage of the fact that August is finishing on a high note. At the same time it's worth demonstrating just how sensitive you can be, and with Venus in your solar seventh house you could prove to be the perfect partner.

31 TUESDAY ☿ *Moon Age Day 21 Moon Sign Taurus*

am . . . .

pm . . . .
In practical matters you need to have a strategy, and you may not be too happy at present if you have to make up your mind on the spur of the moment. This is unusual for Aries, leading to some discomfort if you are not fully in charge of each moment. A little reliance on your intuition may be the sensible answer.

1 WEDNESDAY ☿ *Moon Age Day 22 Moon Sign Gemini*

am . . . .

pm . . . .
On the first day of September, trends encourage you to seek out the help and encouragement of others in almost any situation. You can afford to be quite trusting and shouldn't expect anyone to let you down. Confidence is also high in your work, and this is an ideal time to show superiors how clever you really are.

2 THURSDAY ☿ *Moon Age Day 23 Moon Sign Gemini*

am . . . .

pm . . . .
Communication with others and frank exchanges of opinion remain central to your current success, though you need to beware any tendency to lose your temper under present trends. This becomes more likely if you think those around you are being deliberately stupid, because you don't suffer fools gladly.

3 FRIDAY ☿ *Moon Age Day 24   Moon Sign Cancer*

am . . . .

pm . . . .
The Moon is now in your solar fourth house and whilst it remains there the spotlight is on your home and family. Domestic issues are to the fore for most of the day, and you may decide that the practical side of life has to take a back seat. You have scope to be quite analytical across the next few days.

4 SATURDAY ☿ *Moon Age Day 25   Moon Sign Cancer*

am . . . .

pm . . . .
Your strength lies in making life work in your favour, even if you don't feel you have been putting in very much effort. Although some situations may be a response to things you did earlier, you can also harness a high level of good luck. Why not respond to the kindness of your partner by spoiling them in some specific way?

5 SUNDAY ☿ *Moon Age Day 26   Moon Sign Leo*

am . . . .

pm . . . .
Today is about making personal relationships run smoothly and getting your ideas accepted by those around you. This is a good time to arrange social gatherings, especially those that bring relatives and friends together in the same place. It isn't difficult to realise that you are popular and loved.

September 2010

YOUR MONTH AT A GLANCE

⊕ = Opportunities are around   ⊖ = Be on the defensive   ⬤ = Life is pretty ordinary

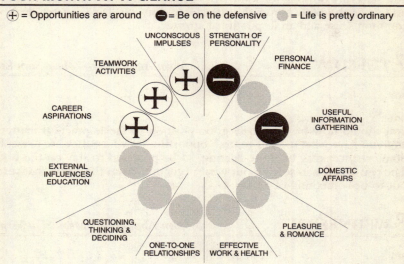

UNCONSCIOUS IMPULSES

STRENGTH OF PERSONALITY

TEAMWORK ACTIVITIES

PERSONAL FINANCE

CAREER ASPIRATIONS

USEFUL INFORMATION GATHERING

EXTERNAL INFLUENCES/ EDUCATION

DOMESTIC AFFAIRS

QUESTIONING, THINKING & DECIDING

PLEASURE & ROMANCE

ONE-TO-ONE RELATIONSHIPS

EFFECTIVE WORK & HEALTH

SEPTEMBER HIGHS AND LOWS

Here I show you how the rhythms of the Moon will affect you this month. Like the tide, your energies and abilities will rise and fall with its pattern. When it is above the centre line, go for it, when it is below, you should be resting.

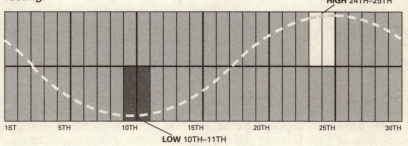

HIGH 24TH–25TH

1ST   5TH   10TH   15TH   20TH   25TH   30TH

LOW 10TH–11TH

121

6 MONDAY   ☿   *Moon Age Day 27   Moon Sign Leo*

am . . . .

pm . . . .
What you might refer to as the 'feel good factor' seems to be present
today. This is likely to be especially the case in personal relationships, and
new starts are possible for some Aries subjects. Your love life can certainly
bring out the best in you this week, but you also have a great deal of
common sense and an inspirational attitude.

7 TUESDAY   ☿   *Moon Age Day 28   Moon Sign Leo*

am . . . .

pm . . . .
You should now be in a really good position to tackle practical matters
and you have what it takes to grab opportunities whilst they are present.
Some chances may be quite fleeting, so be prepared to stay on the ball.
The real skill lies in sorting out what is genuine from the offers that turn
out to be something of a con.

8 WEDNESDAY   ☿   *Moon Age Day 0   Moon Sign Virgo*

am . . . .

pm . . . .
Look out for the kind of personalities who you would like to bring into
your life now. These are probably people who make you feel good to be
alive and who are willing to do almost anything to make you happy. It is
easy to respond positively to such individuals, but you also need to be
enthusiastic with less progressive types.

9 THURSDAY   ☿   *Moon Age Day 1   Moon Sign Virgo*

am . . . .

pm . . . .
This may not be the most inspiring day of the month, but there are still
positive aspects around. Finances can be strengthened, and there are
possible gains to be made from the direction of family members. It might
be slightly difficult fitting in all the responsibilities that are coming your
way as the lunar low starts to bite.

10 FRIDAY ☿ *Moon Age Day 2   Moon Sign Libra*

am . . . .

pm . . . .
Perhaps you need to change a dreary routine or else pep up your social life once the cares of the working day are out of the way. This would be an ideal approach whilst the lunar low is present, otherwise you could end up being pessimistic for no real reason. Keep looking to the medium- and long-term future today.

11 SATURDAY ☿ *Moon Age Day 3   Moon Sign Libra*

am . . . .

pm . . . .
Even if the start of the weekend doesn't turn out to be too sparkling, much depends on the amount of effort you are willing to put in. Rather than getting involved in family arguments, why not get everyone involved in projects that are both useful and fun? As the day wears on you can afford to feel more positive about yourself and your life.

12 SUNDAY ☿ *Moon Age Day 4   Moon Sign Scorpio*

am . . . .

pm . . . .
There are signs that close ties and emotional attachments can supply you with a great deal of enjoyment today. You can make this a real family Sunday when you are happy to talk to your nearest and dearest about things that sometimes get forgotten in the hustle and bustle of everyday life. A day to go with the flow in most matters.

13 MONDAY ☿ *Moon Age Day 5   Moon Sign Scorpio*

am . . . .

pm . . . .
Right now you can be at your very best when it comes to the practical side of life. It's a case of knowing how to get things moving and putting yourself forward when new projects are in the offing. Just don't crowd your schedule so much that you leave yourself with no time to sort anything out properly. Limit your efforts.

14 TUESDAY *Moon Age Day 6   Moon Sign Sagittarius*

am . . . .

pm . . . .
There's nothing wrong with having a busy life at the moment, though you might have to put certain aspects of your social life on hold. It's all very well you being good company, but there are only so many hours in a day. It's worth devoting some of these to your career and to the responsibilities you face in your home life.

15 WEDNESDAY *Moon Age Day 7   Moon Sign Sagittarius*

am . . . .

pm . . . .
If you are feeling emotionally pressured at the moment, ask yourself whether it's because you are taking matters more seriously than you should. Try to relax and also see the funny side of situations – even if they look less than humorous at first. In a career sense Aries should be on a roll, and you can make great headway.

16 THURSDAY *Moon Age Day 8   Moon Sign Capricorn*

am . . . .

pm . . . .
There is much to be said for looking for influential figures and sorting out those who are in a good position to help you out in some way. Facing certain superiors at work could be like being in the Dragon's Den, but being born of the sign of Aries you are equal to any challenge. Let your personality come shining through today.

17 FRIDAY
Moon Age Day 9   Moon Sign Capricorn

am . . . .

pm . . . .
Practical matters can help you get the very best from your life under present trends, and you may not have time to deal with trivial situations. The problem is that what looks inconsequential to you could be of supreme importance to someone else. It is important to judge every situation on its true merits, and that takes intuition.

18 SATURDAY
Moon Age Day 10   Moon Sign Capricorn

am . . . .

pm . . . .
The Moon is now in your solar eleventh house and this is a trend that is best enjoyed in the company of your friends. If the weekend offers you some free time, it's worth spending this with individuals you know well and like a great deal. Try not to put yourself alongside people you find tiring and difficult to deal with.

19 SUNDAY
Moon Age Day 11   Moon Sign Aquarius

am . . . .

pm . . . .
Today's trends highlight a desire to get things done as quickly as possible. This might be an advantage under most circumstances, but could prove to be something of a trial on a Sunday. If there is any good weather left you may decide to spend time out of doors in the company of your partner. At the very least, enjoy social prospects.

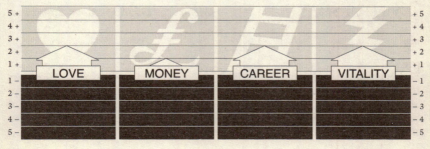

20 MONDAY

Moon Age Day 12   Moon Sign Aquarius

am . . . .

pm . . . .
There should be little difficulty in getting through whatever tasks you have set yourself for today. You can be very disciplined at the best of times, and can use this trait to get through jobs in half the time it would take others. Watch out for a little envy from the direction of people who are far less motivated than you are.

21 TUESDAY

Moon Age Day 13   Moon Sign Pisces

am . . . .

pm . . . .
When you are not doing all you can to further your own interests at work you might decide to pep up your social life in some way. This might involve new groups of people or activities you haven't tried before. Just remember that there doesn't have to be an end-gain in everything you do. Sometimes having fun is quite enough!

22 WEDNESDAY

Moon Age Day 14   Moon Sign Pisces

am . . . .

pm . . . .
Stand by to cut loose some of the dead wood from your life. Mars is now in your solar eighth house and whilst it is there you have the opportunity to really sort things out. This is an ideal time to make some changes, and once you have addressed these you can concentrate more on those aspects of life that are permanent and solid.

23 THURSDAY

Moon Age Day 15   Moon Sign Pisces

am . . . .

pm . . . .
Much of what you can achieve today depends on you clearing the decks for actions that are due tomorrow and beyond. It might seem as if you actually get little or nothing done that is final, but this period of preparation is essential. A contemplative approach is no bad thing whilst the Moon is in your solar twelfth house.

24 FRIDAY
Moon Age Day 16   Moon Sign Aries

am . . . .

pm . . . .

This is the best day of the month to finalise details and to get new incentives going. By all means seek assistance if you need it, though you have what it takes to plough your own furrow just at the moment. Getting Lady Luck on your side assists you to take the sort of chances even you might usually avoid.

25 SATURDAY
Moon Age Day 17   Moon Sign Aries

am . . . .

pm . . . .

Make the most of situations today that offer you a distinct advantage over competitors. This is another legacy of the lunar high and should not be ignored. Look out for the chance to bring new personalities into your life around now, and also make the best of any social invitations that will help you to bring sparkle to the weekend.

26 SUNDAY
Moon Age Day 18   Moon Sign Taurus

am . . . .

pm . . . .

Aries can make the world an easy place to live in under present planetary trends. The Sun is now in your solar seventh house, where it will remain for the next three or four weeks. You can benefit from romantic attachments, and should be quite happy to meet and greet all manner of new people who appear around now.

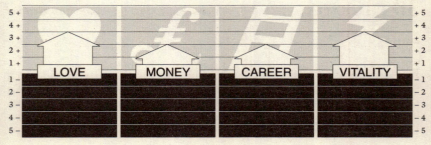

27 MONDAY
Moon Age Day 19   Moon Sign Taurus

am . . . .

pm . . . .
A little soul-searching may be in order as you attempt to come to terms with certain aspects of your daily life. There are good reasons to analyse situations, and there is also an indication that this is an ideal time for getting rid of any baggage you have been carrying around for a very long time.

28 TUESDAY
Moon Age Day 20   Moon Sign Taurus

am . . . .

pm . . . .
A phase of extreme productivity can now be achieved. There are favourable trends around for those who work full time and it isn't out of the question that a new offer will be forthcoming. By all means take your responsibilities seriously, though you may also decide to find moments when you can lighten the load somewhat.

29 WEDNESDAY
Moon Age Day 21   Moon Sign Gemini

am . . . .

pm . . . .
This ought to be a good time for negotiations or deals of one sort or another. You can be quite impressive to others, especially if you show them you are both organised and authoritative. All the same, it is important not to come across as being too bossy. This is an aspect of your Aries nature that is sometimes difficult to avoid.

30 THURSDAY
Moon Age Day 22   Moon Sign Gemini

am . . . .

pm . . . .
A good deal of mental energy is available as the week wears on and much of it can be ploughed into your work. All the same, you need moments to play, and have scope to persuade others to join in with the fun. Even if this proves impossible during the day, it's worth thinking up some ways to brighten the evening.

1 FRIDAY
Moon Age Day 23   Moon Sign Cancer

am . . . .

pm . . . .
Now the focus is on a concern with matters of personal security. The Moon is in your solar fourth house and this also encourages you to look more closely at domestic issues and the well-being of your family. With the weekend in view, this is an ideal time for you to bring both balance and flair to your life.

2 SATURDAY
Moon Age Day 24   Moon Sign Cancer

am . . . .

pm . . . .
The practical solutions you dream up when dealing with day-to-day problems can be quite inspirational. Certainly you have what it takes to make those around you take notice and be quite envious of your talents. It's good to attract compliments, and it is really important that you learn to recognise them.

3 SUNDAY
Moon Age Day 25   Moon Sign Leo

am . . . .

pm . . . .
Partnerships can now be boosted by better communication skills on your part. It is sometimes the case that Aries people are so busy they fail to say the most important things. To do so takes only a few seconds, and the odd compliment can prove to be extremely important, especially in the case of your partner or much loved friends.

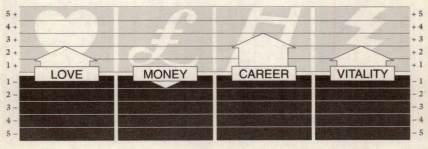

October 2010

YOUR MONTH AT A GLANCE

⊕ = Opportunities are around   ⊖ = Be on the defensive   ⬤ = Life is pretty ordinary

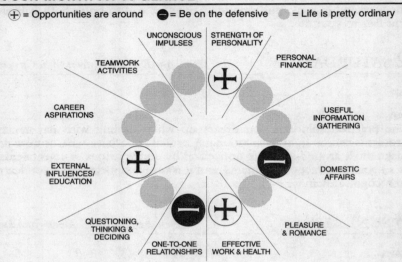

UNCONSCIOUS IMPULSES

STRENGTH OF PERSONALITY

TEAMWORK ACTIVITIES

PERSONAL FINANCE

CAREER ASPIRATIONS

USEFUL INFORMATION GATHERING

EXTERNAL INFLUENCES/ EDUCATION

DOMESTIC AFFAIRS

QUESTIONING, THINKING & DECIDING

ONE-TO-ONE RELATIONSHIPS

EFFECTIVE WORK & HEALTH

PLEASURE & ROMANCE

OCTOBER HIGHS AND LOWS

Here I show you how the rhythms of the Moon will affect you this month. Like the tide, your energies and abilities will rise and fall with its pattern. When it is above the centre line, go for it, when it is below, you should be resting.

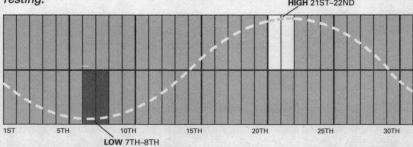

HIGH 21ST–22ND

1ST   5TH   10TH   15TH   20TH   25TH   30TH

LOW 7TH–8TH

4 MONDAY

Moon Age Day 26   Moon Sign Leo

am . . . .

pm . . . .
You can make this a fairly smooth time from a social point of view. It's all about getting situations to arrange themselves and finding people to rely on. The really warm side of your nature is emphasised, assisting you to make those close to you happy. At work you might have to be just a little circumspect at times.

5 TUESDAY

Moon Age Day 27   Moon Sign Virgo

am . . . .

pm . . . .
For once you may choose to ignore responsibilities, though this trend is caused by the quick-moving Moon so it shouldn't last long. For now you can afford to let others make some of the decisions, whilst you watch, wait and meditate. Anything that doesn't get done today can be dealt with later, so why not enjoy a little break?

6 WEDNESDAY

Moon Age Day 28   Moon Sign Virgo

am . . . .

pm . . . .
This would be a fabulous time for partnerships. The Sun is in your solar seventh house, and there is more than a little good luck available when you are dealing with co-operative ventures. When it comes to getting on with practical tasks you can be on top form, and your dexterity is almost worthy of a medal right now.

7 THURSDAY

Moon Age Day 29   Moon Sign Libra

am . . . .

pm . . . .
The lunar low could urge you to drop a few responsibilities, even though a part of your nature knows that this is not the right way to proceed. What you might have to do for the next couple of days is to prioritise more than usual. 'One job at once' will be the rule, and taking frequent breaks from responsibility is the order of the day.

8 FRIDAY

Moon Age Day 0   Moon Sign Libra

am . . . .

pm . . . .
You might feel as if others are getting ahead quicker than you are, and
some frustration could arise if you seem to be dropping behind. Don't
worry, because only a few hours into tomorrow you can make sure you
are fully on form again. Actually you can make this a very happy and
comfortable day if you put your mind to it.

9 SATURDAY

Moon Age Day 1   Moon Sign Scorpio

am . . . .

pm . . . .
That very progressive and competitive Aries nature can be put on display
again today, which just goes to show how temporary the lunar low can
be. Even the arrival of the weekend needn't prevent you from taking
steps to push ahead. Even if you can't do anything concrete, you can at
least plan moves for later.

10 SUNDAY

Moon Age Day 2   Moon Sign Scorpio

am . . . .

pm . . . .
Though you may not intend to do so, there is a chance that you will
allow others to overshadow you in some way. Maybe you are not thinking
clearly enough about your strategies or perhaps taking on so much you
can't do everything equally well. You probably won't take kindly to being
beaten into second place in any situation.

11 MONDAY
Moon Age Day 3   Moon Sign Sagittarius

am . . . .

pm . . . .
The present position of the Moon suggests a need to wander and a sort of dreaminess that is usually fairly alien to your nature. Focusing your attention may be difficult, and you may also decide to plan activities that have nothing to do with the practical or financial side of your life. In some ways this could be a good thing.

12 TUESDAY
Moon Age Day 4   Moon Sign Sagittarius

am . . . .

pm . . . .
Attracting people you meet in casual situations is a natural aspect of today, though of course this isn't too odd because your nature can be very magnetic. The amount of attention you bring upon yourself may even prove to be slightly embarrassing on occasions. Be prepared to fend people off if necessary!

13 WEDNESDAY
Moon Age Day 5   Moon Sign Sagittarius

am . . . .

pm . . . .
There is better scope today for professional advancement and you have what it takes to be on the ball when it comes to getting things done. Whilst others are standing and thinking about their next move, you may already have made yours and will be on to the next venture. In personal attachments it's time to show your charisma.

14 THURSDAY
Moon Age Day 6   Moon Sign Capricorn

am . . . .

pm . . . .
There may well be a whole boatload of emotional stresses to be dealt with at this time, and you need to be very careful not to overstretch yourself when it comes to relationships. If you have more than one iron in the romantic fire, life could get very complicated. It might be best to settle for what is safe and fairly ordinary.

15 FRIDAY
Moon Age Day 7   Moon Sign Capricorn

am . . . .

pm . . . .
Joint ventures and pursuits are the ones to follow whilst the Sun remains in its present position in your solar chart. If there are occasions when it seems to take ages to get the simplest task out of the way, your best approach is to be prepared to share the glory with anyone who is willing to share the work.

16 SATURDAY
Moon Age Day 8   Moon Sign Aquarius

am . . . .

pm . . . .
In a social sense you can create plenty of light-hearted moments around now. These seem to be just what you need and can help you lift your spirits no end. Avoid getting hold of the wrong end of the stick when it comes to a romantic matter. It's worth explaining yourself fully before you commit to any course of action.

17 SUNDAY
Moon Age Day 9   Moon Sign Aquarius

am . . . .

pm . . . .
Now is the time to get rid of anything that is superficial and outdated, because you can't afford to be carrying too much luggage around. Stick to what is essential to your life and give up thoughts of achieving anything that seems virtually impossible. This is only a temporary state of affairs – because the impossible is usually your forte!

18 MONDAY   *Moon Age Day 10   Moon Sign Aquarius*

am . . . .

pm . . . .
You have an innate ability to make snap decisions, but for once you may
be at a loss to understand all the implications of the possibilities that
surround you. Trends suggest a slight lack of confidence, something you
don't deal with very well. Even if you aren't exactly panicking at the
moment, you may not be on top form either.

19 TUESDAY   *Moon Age Day 11   Moon Sign Pisces*

am . . . .

pm . . . .
Whilst the Moon occupies your solar twelfth house it would be sensible
to get some relaxation and to enjoy what your home life and friendship
have to offer. You should soon have scope to bring new personalities into
your life, but for the moment it's worth sticking to people you know –
and especially family members.

20 WEDNESDAY   *Moon Age Day 12   Moon Sign Pisces*

am . . . .

pm . . . .
Today is about creating a warm glow when it comes to personal
attachments. You can achieve this by spending time monitoring what is
going on and how others feel. As a rule you are probably so busy dashing
from pillar to post that you tend to be ignorant of certain atmospheres.
You could also discover a secret admirer right now.

21 THURSDAY   *Moon Age Day 13   Moon Sign Aries*

am . . . .

pm . . . .
The lunar high is the best time of the month for making new starts, and
you need to dispel all the negativity associated with that twelfth-house
Moon. If you know what you want, your level of good luck is such that
you can also work out how to get it. Convincing others should be a piece
of cake today.

22 FRIDAY
Moon Age Day 14   Moon Sign Aries

am . . . .

pm . . . .
Mixing with successful people would be no bad thing, because some of their potential is likely to rub off on you. Surprises are possible today, but most of these should be fortunate, and there are times when you have a chance to shine like the Sun itself. Confidence attends new activities, but any sort of nostalgia is less positive.

23 SATURDAY
Moon Age Day 15   Moon Sign Aries

am . . . .

pm . . . .
A phase of continued change and transformation should keep you very much on your toes. In addition to the lunar high the Sun is now entering your solar eighth house and this offers great diversity and the chance to make alterations in your life. You should be dealing with the fantastic potential of this period by reacting positively.

24 SUNDAY
Moon Age Day 16   Moon Sign Taurus

am . . . .

pm . . . .
Whilst some slight caution is now wise in terms of your finances, in other ways you can keep life speeding on very positively. Whether or not others can keep up with the pace you are setting remains to be seen, and even in a social sense it is possible that you will spend a good part of today waiting around for others to catch up.

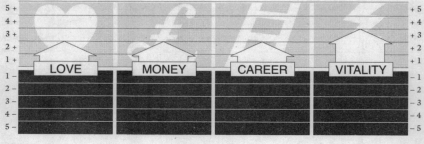

25 MONDAY · *Moon Age Day 17* · *Moon Sign Taurus*

am . . . .

pm . . . .
A favourable time to think and study. Those Aries subjects who are involved in education could be the luckiest of all because your ability to take in new information has rarely been better. This might mean that you decide not to be quite as physical in your actions as you would wish to be. A steady attitude works best now.

26 TUESDAY · *Moon Age Day 18* · *Moon Sign Gemini*

am . . . .

pm . . . .
It's worth examining any project or idea for the future in minute detail. That eighth-house Sun definitely offers change but it also demands that you know what you are doing. Rushing headlong into just about any situation is to be avoided, and there is much to be said for calling on the resources of professionals at this time.

27 WEDNESDAY · *Moon Age Day 19* · *Moon Sign Gemini*

am . . . .

pm . . . .
This is a period when change is possible, but also one that allows you to review some of your past actions. This in turn could lead to nostalgia, which is probably best avoided. The eighth-house Sun urges action, but it can also encourage you to look too deeply into your own psychological motivations. Try to stay light and casual.

28 THURSDAY · *Moon Age Day 20* · *Moon Sign Cancer*

am . . . .

pm . . . .
If many of your present concerns revolve around family members, it might be best to ask them what they think. As an Aries subject you tend to believe you know best for everyone, but this isn't always the case. A good heart-to-heart with your partner or family members should keep them feeling that their opinions are being considered.

29 FRIDAY
Moon Age Day 21   Moon Sign Cancer

am . . . .

pm . . . .
You can achieve a high degree of intimacy under present trends, and today and over the weekend ahead you can use this to move closer to someone special than you have felt yourself to be for quite some time. It is important not to lose touch with your roots or with the motivations that brought you to where you are right now.

30 SATURDAY
Moon Age Day 22   Moon Sign Cancer

am . . . .

pm . . . .
Today is about dispensing with the superficial or irrelevant, and that's fine, just as long as you don't throw out the baby with the bathwater. You would be wise to think carefully before you make any major decisions, and your usual strategy of acting and then wondering after whether it was the right thing simply won't do.

31 SUNDAY
Moon Age Day 23   Moon Sign Leo

am . . . .

pm . . . .
Beware of coming across as a know-it-all today. Even if inside yourself you are feeling fairly modest and even humble at present, that may not be the way you seem to be when viewed by others. Such is the power of Aries that you can sometimes swamp people and situations without any intention at all of doing so.

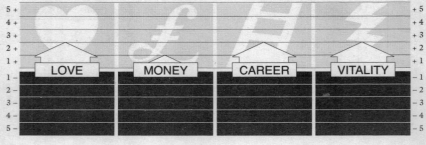

November

2010

YOUR MONTH AT A GLANCE

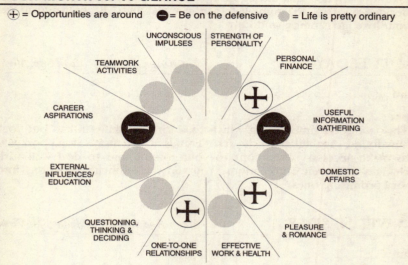

⊕ = Opportunities are around   ⊖ = Be on the defensive   ● = Life is pretty ordinary

- UNCONSCIOUS IMPULSES
- STRENGTH OF PERSONALITY
- TEAMWORK ACTIVITIES
- PERSONAL FINANCE ⊕
- CAREER ASPIRATIONS ⊖
- USEFUL INFORMATION GATHERING ⊖
- EXTERNAL INFLUENCES/ EDUCATION
- DOMESTIC AFFAIRS
- QUESTIONING, THINKING & DECIDING
- ONE-TO-ONE RELATIONSHIPS ⊕
- EFFECTIVE WORK & HEALTH
- PLEASURE & ROMANCE

NOVEMBER HIGHS AND LOWS

Here I show you how the rhythms of the Moon will affect you this month. Like the tide, your energies and abilities will rise and fall with its pattern. When it is above the centre line, go for it, when it is below, you should be resting.

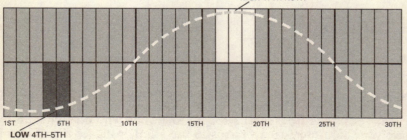

HIGH 17TH–19TH

1ST   5TH   10TH   15TH   20TH   25TH   30TH

LOW 4TH–5TH

1 MONDAY
Moon Age Day 24   Moon Sign Leo

am . . . .

pm . . . .
Don't be too quick to make up your mind today. There are many options facing you and it is essential that you are sure of any action before you take it. Why not seek advice from someone you trust? Once you have decided what to do, immediate action works best. Be prepared to get your love life running smoothly.

2 TUESDAY
Moon Age Day 25   Moon Sign Virgo

am . . . .

pm . . . .
This is a good time during which to learn new skills and to put your new-found capabilities to the test. Trends at the moment support you to make necessary alterations to your routine and to deal well with changes and even cancellations. You can turn difficult situations into very promising ones.

3 WEDNESDAY
Moon Age Day 26   Moon Sign Virgo

am . . . .

pm . . . .
This is a time to be patient with yourself. The lunar low arrives before the end of the day, and you may not have either your usual resilience or energy. Your best approach is to let others take the strain, whilst you make the decisions and supervise. Today is about clear thinking and a degree of circumspection.

4 THURSDAY
Moon Age Day 27   Moon Sign Libra

am . . . .

pm . . . .
Now is the time to focus on what is positive rather than on awkward or negative situations. This might sound quite easy, but could be quite a trial on occasions. Your ideal response to anyone who doesn't seem to have your best interests at heart is to use a little patience to talk them round to your point of view.

5 FRIDAY
Moon Age Day 28   Moon Sign Libra

am . . . .

pm . . . .
If things are not going well for any reason you can at least tell yourself that tomorrow is another day. The end of the working week could be attended by obstacles of one sort or another and it is the way you deal with these that shows your mettle. Don't get caught up in pointless discussions about matters you can't either control or alter.

6 SATURDAY
Moon Age Day 0   Moon Sign Scorpio

am . . . .

pm . . . .
Trends promote a fascination with anything personal, sensitive or secret today. Keeping confidences is the order of the day, whether it's the secrets of friends or your own innermost thoughts. In amongst this rather peculiar period you can find islands of entertainment and can improve your social life in a surprising way.

7 SUNDAY
Moon Age Day 1   Moon Sign Scorpio

am . . . .

pm . . . .
You should be really at home now when it comes to solving problems. You have what it takes to think deeply about everything under present trends and to make change your middle name. However, that doesn't mean altering things simply for the sake of doing so. Casual attachments can be turned into something much deeper now.

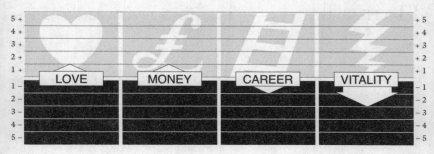

8 MONDAY
Moon Age Day 2   Moon Sign Sagittarius

am . . . .

pm . . . .
The time is right to seek out people and situations that can broaden your horizons. Take the opportunity to travel to new and unexplored places and to find out things you didn't know before. Your mind has few limits under present trends and it can be amazing just how much information you can take in during one short day.

9 TUESDAY
Moon Age Day 3   Moon Sign Sagittarius

am . . . .

pm . . . .
There is a high degree of change and diversity on offer around now. Much of this is thanks to the Sun in your solar eighth house. Take advantage of new and inspirational ideas and also of the assistance offered by people who really know their onions. Romance is also well starred under present trends, so be prepared to seek affection.

10 WEDNESDAY
Moon Age Day 4   Moon Sign Capricorn

am . . . .

pm . . . .
Though the general accent is now upon getting things done, there's nothing wrong with being a little circumspect. You have what it takes to think very deeply about relationships and to work out the best way to renew your commitment to the person who is most important in your life. You may even be quite poetical at the moment.

11 THURSDAY
Moon Age Day 5   Moon Sign Capricorn

am . . . .

pm . . . .
You exude an aura of grace and good taste, and can use this to attract other people. As an Aries subject you know how to behave in company, and at the moment you shouldn't be stuck for the right thing to say. If you manage to get yourself into elevated company, don't be afraid to put forward your opinions to all.

12 FRIDAY

Moon Age Day 6   Moon Sign Capricorn

am . . . .

pm . . . .
Now you can benefit from having something new and interesting to say at every turn. Your practical resources know no bounds, and it should be easy to get more than one job out of the way at the same time. This would be a good time to go shopping, especially to a town or district you don't visit very often.

13 SATURDAY

Moon Age Day 7   Moon Sign Aquarius

am . . . .

pm . . . .
At the moment you can afford to be kinder and more tolerant than ever, and can make sure your popularity is going off the scale. Why not use the weekend to have fun and get to know someone much better? It's all about building a larger circle of friends and acquaintances, some of whom will become increasingly important to you.

14 SUNDAY

Moon Age Day 8   Moon Sign Aquarius

am . . . .

pm . . . .
It looks as though you may now be more susceptible to outside influences. The Moon is entering your solar twelfth house, emphasising your ability to be circumspect. It isn't necessary to brood over situations, but glossing over them isn't the answer either. With balance you can turn this into a very useful day.

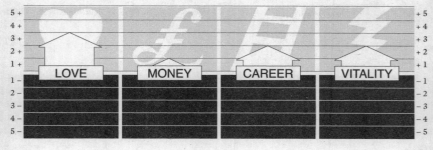

15 MONDAY

Moon Age Day 9   Moon Sign Pisces

am . . . .

pm . . . .
Romantic affairs are now positively highlighted because Venus is in such a good position in your solar chart. Getting your own way with others at the moment is largely a matter of turning on the charm, and there should be no need to fall out with anyone. Look out for a new opportunity to really shine in your workplace.

16 TUESDAY

Moon Age Day 10   Moon Sign Pisces

am . . . .

pm . . . .
Even if emotional attachments are putting great demands on both your time and your energy, bear in mind that they may well be the most important components of your life today. By all means find time to get practical things done, but in the main the focus is on love and the positive part it presently plays in your life.

17 WEDNESDAY

Moon Age Day 11   Moon Sign Aries

am . . . .

pm . . . .
The lunar high is the ideal time to make new starts and to solidify plans that are now beginning to mature. There are new incentives available too, and you shouldn't be tardy when it comes to making gains from these. Beware of taking on more work than you need to, because there is more than enough to get through as it is.

18 THURSDAY

Moon Age Day 12   Moon Sign Aries

am . . . .

pm . . . .
Prepare to make fresh starts and to take some chances. Aries should be at its decisive best, and there are few people around who could presently rival you for energy or perseverance. On the way through your day you can identify people who may well turn out to be extremely important in a few weeks.

19 FRIDAY   *Moon Age Day 13   Moon Sign Aries*

am . . . .

pm . . . .

The day's events make it easy for you to be original and to experience a number of breakthroughs when it matters the most. Any difficulties that have been hanging around in your life for a while can now be sorted out quickly and efficiently, and you can really fire on all cylinders in your desire to make special headway at work.

20 SATURDAY   *Moon Age Day 14   Moon Sign Taurus*

am . . . .

pm . . . .

This ought to be a particularly encouraging time for travel. Although the days are getting shorter and the winter is at hand, you could make real gains from moving around more. It isn't out of the question that some Aries people will choose this time for a holiday. If you are one of them, don't forget to pack the essentials.

21 SUNDAY   *Moon Age Day 15   Moon Sign Taurus*

am . . . .

pm . . . .

Don't be surprised if you now encounter issues that demand a degree of discussion. The main word of warning is not to allow these to become arguments. Aries is not noted for its patience and you don't suffer fools at all gladly. It would be better for all concerned if you were to bite your tongue and show a high degree of patience.

22 MONDAY
Moon Age Day 16   Moon Sign Gemini

am . . . .

pm . . . .
This would be a really good time to take a different and perhaps ultimately a more stimulating approach to discussions. These could well be of a practical nature and may not have the domestic overtones that were indicated for yesterday. If the attitude of a friend puzzles you, there's nothing wrong with asking a few questions.

23 TUESDAY
Moon Age Day 17   Moon Sign Gemini

am . . . .

pm . . . .
This is a day during which freedom may appear to be the most important factor. You may not take kindly to being restricted in any way, and could well fight tenaciously if you suspect that someone is trying to get the better of you. Routines are not for you just now, and you shouldn't be afraid to make up your mind as you go along.

24 WEDNESDAY
Moon Age Day 18   Moon Sign Gemini

am . . . .

pm . . . .
Look towards positive highlights in personal relationships and a new approach to romance. Trends assist you to sweep others off their feet, and encourage you to use your curious mind. Nothing should be beneath your attention, and finding out what makes everything in the world tick is a natural part of life now.

25 THURSDAY
Moon Age Day 19   Moon Sign Cancer

am . . . .

pm . . . .
Freedom of movement is more vital than ever. Little Mercury is now in your solar ninth house, as indeed is the Sun. Travel allows you to broaden your horizons, and seeking opportunities to make journeys would be no bad thing. Something quite exotic could be in the offing, and you make full use of the good luck on offer.

26 FRIDAY
Moon Age Day 20   Moon Sign Cancer

am . . . .

pm . . . .
This would be an ideal time to get involved in philosophical discussions. Your mind runs deep and you can use it to please those with whom you come into contact. You can afford to show other people that you are intelligent and good to know. Once again, tedious routines may not seem to be your most attractive option.

27 SATURDAY
Moon Age Day 21   Moon Sign Leo

am . . . .

pm . . . .
A high-spirited time is on offer. This would be a good time to do something quite different and to find ways to both surprise and please your partner. Those Aries subjects who are between relationships at the moment can turn this into a very special weekend. All you have to do is to keep your eyes open.

28 SUNDAY
Moon Age Day 22   Moon Sign Leo

am . . . .

pm . . . .
Getting to grips with issues that have puzzled or troubled you in the past should be possible today. There are times when the way ahead looks clear to the horizon, and this could well be one of them. If standard responses don't work when dealing with younger family members, perhaps the time has come to show some originality.

29 MONDAY
Moon Age Day 23   Moon Sign Virgo

am . . . .

pm . . . .
Relating to others in a personal sense has rarely been so easy or potentially enjoyable as it is now. Confidence remains essentially high, and you can take advantage of some exciting surprises if you keep your eyes open. Even if not everything that comes your way is intended for you, you have a good ability to be in the best place to benefit.

30 TUESDAY
Moon Age Day 24   Moon Sign Virgo

am . . . .

pm . . . .
Work developments are positively highlighted under present trends and this is a week during which you can make a great deal of headway, especially with any matters that have been troublesome in the past. Things that took you ages to sort out before should now become a piece of cake, particularly if you use new techniques and shortcuts.

1 WEDNESDAY
Moon Age Day 25   Moon Sign Libra

am . . . .

pm . . . .
The first day of December brings the lunar low and a period of possible reversals unless you are well prepared. Beware of reacting too strongly to situations that might resolve themselves if you simply leave them alone. Pushing against immovable situations is not to be recommended, but a higher degree of patience certainly is.

2 THURSDAY
Moon Age Day 26   Moon Sign Libra

am . . . .

pm . . . .
Right now you should be prepared to let others make the running. Trends suggest a time of uncharacteristic laziness, and you might not even want to get out of bed this morning. Your best approach is to avoid getting depressed by matters that are not at all important and to show resolve if you have to deal with family members.

3 FRIDAY

Moon Age Day 27   Moon Sign Scorpio

am . . . .

pm . . . .
The lunar low passes away and now you can tap into the power of the Sun. Intellectual growth becomes possible, and you have what it takes to get things to work out to your advantage. Now is the time to show your cultured side and to revel in the company of people who can offer you fascinating conversations.

4 SATURDAY

Moon Age Day 28   Moon Sign Scorpio

am . . . .

pm . . . .
This may be one of the best times in December for emotional attachments and for proving to someone very special that they are central to your life. In the busy life that Aries leads there isn't always sufficient time for compliments and presents, but you have what it takes right now to make someone fall in love with you even more.

5 SUNDAY

Moon Age Day 29   Moon Sign Sagittarius

am . . . .

pm . . . .
Even if there is a degree of restlessness to be dealt with today, this can be used to your advantage. This is not a day to be standing still, or worse still to be sitting around in front of the television. Use your creative potential to better advantage and get involved in projects that will give you satisfaction throughout the winter.

♈ December 2010

YOUR MONTH AT A GLANCE

⊕ = Opportunities are around   ⊖ = Be on the defensive   ◯ = Life is pretty ordinary

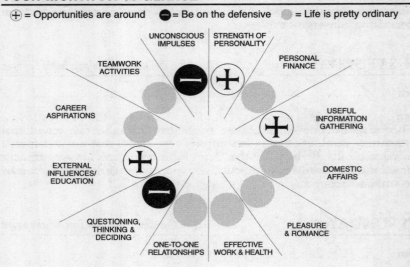

UNCONSCIOUS IMPULSES ⊖
STRENGTH OF PERSONALITY ⊕
TEAMWORK ACTIVITIES
PERSONAL FINANCE
CAREER ASPIRATIONS
USEFUL INFORMATION GATHERING ⊕
EXTERNAL INFLUENCES/EDUCATION ⊕
DOMESTIC AFFAIRS
QUESTIONING, THINKING & DECIDING ⊖
PLEASURE & ROMANCE
ONE-TO-ONE RELATIONSHIPS
EFFECTIVE WORK & HEALTH

DECEMBER HIGHS AND LOWS

Here I show you how the rhythms of the Moon will affect you this month. Like the tide, your energies and abilities will rise and fall with its pattern. When it is above the centre line, go for it, when it is below, you should be resting.

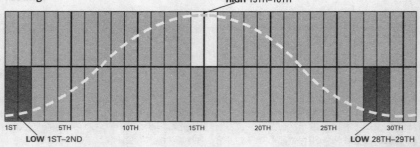

HIGH 15TH–16TH

1ST   5TH   10TH   15TH   20TH   25TH   30TH

LOW 1ST–2ND

LOW 28TH–29TH

6 MONDAY
Moon Age Day 0   Moon Sign Sagittarius

am . . . .

pm . . . .
This would be a good time to renew your energy through pleasurable
mental activities and by associating with people you find stimulating and
fun to be around. You can be very inspiring to know, and can get onside
with new colleagues, especially at work. Be prepared to meet people from
the past who reappear during this period.

7 TUESDAY
Moon Age Day 1   Moon Sign Capricorn

am . . . .

pm . . . .
Even if practical matters are going well enough, you may feel that
something is missing from your life at the moment. Putting in that little
extra effort can make all the difference. Finances can be strengthened
under present trends, particularly if you make sure you are being shrewd
in your judgements.

8 WEDNESDAY
Moon Age Day 2   Moon Sign Capricorn

am . . . .

pm . . . .
Assuming a role of authority isn't hard for Aries and may turn out to be
necessary if you really want to get on well at the present time. There may
be occasions when you feel as though you are somehow 'pretending' to
be in charge, but as long as you can convince others of the role you are
adopting, does your motivation matter?

9 THURSDAY
Moon Age Day 3   Moon Sign Capricorn

am . . . .

pm . . . .
An outgoing approach works well today, and can help you in your efforts
to get on with a whole variety of different people. Even those who have
been difficult to approach in the past should be easier to handle under
present planetary trends, and you have the ability to change like a
chameleon to suit your surroundings.

10 FRIDAY
Moon Age Day 4   Moon Sign Aquarius

am . . . .

pm . . . .
A change of scenery would probably suit you as the working week comes to an end. If you have the chance to get away from everything that is absolutely normal in your life, why not do so? With the weekend in sight it's worth looking at alternatives and new starts. This might be far easier to achieve in a different environment.

11 SATURDAY   ☿   *Moon Age Day 5   Moon Sign Aquarius*

am . . . .

pm . . . .
Passionate relationships and powerful contacts are the order of the day on this particular Saturday. The key is to show exactly the right face to different people, and you should excel in situations that make demands on your flexibility. Don't be afraid to confront a phobia or some sort of problem from the past at this time.

12 SUNDAY   ☿   *Moon Age Day 6   Moon Sign Pisces*

am . . . .

pm . . . .
You would be wise to be just a little more careful than usual when approaching anything new, especially in a physical sense. It is possible that you will be susceptible to injuries, and also that you might be doing more in a physical sense than is good for you. These are trends that are brought about by a twelfth-house Moon.

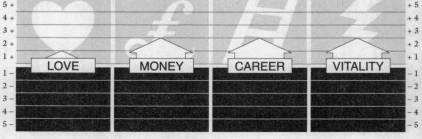

13 MONDAY ☿ *Moon Age Day 7   Moon Sign Pisces*

am . . . .

pm . . . .
If you can stay on the right side of those that matter at work today you will be doing yourself an important favour. In a day or two the astrological circumstances change and you will be able to reap benefits from your conciliatory approach now. Don't do too much today, and leave some spare time to simply sit and think about life.

14 TUESDAY ☿ *Moon Age Day 8   Moon Sign Pisces*

am . . . .

pm . . . .
Trends encourage you to review your recent actions and consider whether you could have done better in some way. Much of this has to do with your present frame of mind, and you can change just about everything negative in your head within a matter of hours. This is not a day to react strongly.

15 WEDNESDAY ☿ *Moon Age Day 9   Moon Sign Aries*

am . . . .

pm . . . .
The lunar high enhances your ability to enlist positive support for any scheme that is important to you, and if you have been keeping people happy for the last few days you can now persuade them to help you out. If rules get in your way today, you have what it takes to find ways to get round them.

16 THURSDAY ☿ *Moon Age Day 10   Moon Sign Aries*

am . . . .

pm . . . .
Now is the time to channel your energies carefully, particularly if there is plenty going on around you today. New incentives and possibilities lie around every corner and you shouldn't have to work too hard in order to get your own way. Be prepared to get Lady Luck on your side and to strengthen your finances.

17 FRIDAY ☿ *Moon Age Day 11* *Moon Sign Taurus*

am . . . .

pm . . . .
The focus is now firmly on hard work, but that shouldn't bother you at
all. You know what you want from life and – typical of Aries – you also
know how to get it. There could be a slightly ruthless streak about you
at the moment, but this isn't especially unusual either. You have scope to
find ways to please your partner later.

18 SATURDAY ☿ *Moon Age Day 12* *Moon Sign Taurus*

am . . . .

pm . . . .
Intimate relationships tend to be your best area today, even if you are still
pushing hard towards practical and professional objectives. People
captivate you with their unique approach, and the way you observe the
world enables you to adopt a more philosophical approach as the day
wears on. Why not get together with friends?

19 SUNDAY ☿ *Moon Age Day 13* *Moon Sign Taurus*

am . . . .

pm . . . .
Because you are born under the sign of Aries, which makes you very
much a creature of the moment, it might only now have occurred to you
that Christmas lies just around the corner. There is much to be said for
getting some shopping out of the way today and for writing all those
cards that you have singularly failed to deal with.

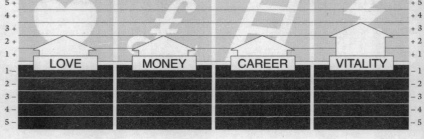

20 MONDAY ☿ *Moon Age Day 14   Moon Sign Gemini*

am . . . .

pm . . . .
Your competitive drive is strong, and so are your instincts. Now you can rely on your own native wit and your ability to put yourself in the best position at the right time. Although advice may be available from others right now, you really need to choose for yourself. Routines won't suit you today and originality is what counts.

21 TUESDAY ☿ *Moon Age Day 15   Moon Sign Gemini*

am . . . .

pm . . . .
With the Sun still in your solar ninth house you have scope to do your own thing, and can use the present force of your personality to counter any interference from others. Despite the fact that you can scare the wits out of some people, to others you can show yourself to be intriguing, kind, considerate and a pussycat to deal with.

22 WEDNESDAY ☿ *Moon Age Day 16   Moon Sign Cancer*

am . . . .

pm . . . .
With Christmas imminent it is possible that there are things to do at home, maybe in order to accommodate whoever is going to turn up for the festivities. Today would be ideal for such preparations, and your strength lies in dealing with all details quickly and efficiently. By the evening you could be falling prey to nostalgia.

23 THURSDAY ☿ *Moon Age Day 17   Moon Sign Cancer*

am . . . .

pm . . . .
A day to use your initiative at work, particularly if you will be slogging away merrily until the last possible moment prior to the holidays. Some Aries subjects will already be starting to burn the candle at both ends but fortunately you are a resilient type and can get away with doing so in the short term. Really talk to family members tonight.

24 FRIDAY ☿ *Moon Age Day 18   Moon Sign Leo*

am . . . .

pm . . . .
There is entertaining company to be had and your winning ways show no
sign of diminishing. You can be a bright and glorious star across the
Christmas period, and for many of you it all begins today. New love is a
possibility for some, whilst others can use the trends to commit
themselves more and more to what they have.

25 SATURDAY ☿ *Moon Age Day 19   Moon Sign Leo*

am . . . .

pm . . . .
If ever there was a day to hog the limelight, this is it for Aries! You are in
a position to make Christmas Day a truly magical time, both for yourself
and for those around you too. True, you might have to play the honest
broker if others fail to get on well, but this shouldn't turn out to be a
problem for you.

26 SUNDAY ☿ *Moon Age Day 20   Moon Sign Virgo*

am . . . .

pm . . . .
You can turn this into a day of comfort and security. Venus is in your solar
eighth house, placing the spotlight on home and family. On balance you
may decide you are happier in your own surroundings than you would be
travelling far and wide. It's also worth finding time to explore the
possibilities of some of those presents.

27 MONDAY ☿ *Moon Age Day 21 Moon Sign Virgo*

am . . . .

pm . . . .
A day to get on with something worthwhile rather than sitting around for too long. The key is to be organised, and to get out and about. Stay in the social mainstream and mix with others.

28 TUESDAY ☿ *Moon Age Day 22 Moon Sign Libra*

am . . . .

pm . . . .
A lower profile is indicated during the lunar low. Spending time on your own shouldn't bother you now. A good time to lay down plans for spring or summer next year. Family trends are positive.

29 WEDNESDAY ☿ *Moon Age Day 23 Moon Sign Libra*

am . . . .

pm . . . .
Counter any tendency to look on the black side by staying optimistic. The time of year isn't to blame for dark thoughts, as tomorrow will show. Focus on the good things in life, not the negatives.

30 THURSDAY ☿ *Moon Age Day 24 Moon Sign Scorpio*

am . . . .

pm . . . .
Vitality may still be lacking early on, though you can change this. By the afternoon you should be raring to go and back on form for the year-end celebrations. There is a focus on the past now.

31 FRIDAY *Moon Age Day 25 Moon Sign Scorpio*

am . . . .

pm . . . .
You needn't let unresolved personal issues get in the way of strong social imperatives and a positive view of practical matters. You have scope to take charge – and to persuade others to allow you that honour.

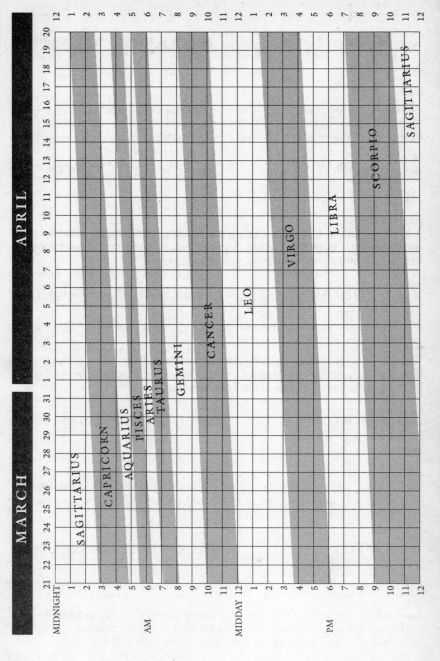

THE ZODIAC, PLANETS AND CORRESPONDENCES

The Earth revolves around the Sun once every calendar year, so when viewed from Earth the Sun appears in a different part of the sky as the year progresses. In astrology, these parts of the sky are divided into the signs of the zodiac and this means that the signs are organised in a circle. The circle begins with Aries and ends with Pisces.

Taking the zodiac sign as a starting point, astrologers then work with all the positions of planets, stars and many other factors to calculate horoscopes and birth charts and tell us what the stars have in store for us.

The table below shows the planets and Elements for each of the signs of the zodiac. Each sign belongs to one of the four Elements: Fire, Air, Earth or Water. Fire signs are creative and enthusiastic; Air signs are mentally active and thoughtful; Earth signs are constructive and practical; Water signs are emotional and have strong feelings.

It also shows the metals and gemstones associated with, or corresponding with, each sign. The correspondence is made when a metal or stone possesses properties that are held in common with a particular sign of the zodiac.

Finally, the table shows the opposite of each star sign – this is the opposite sign in the astrological circle.

Placed	Sign	Symbol	Element	Planet	Metal	Stone	Opposite
1	Aries	Ram	Fire	Mars	Iron	Bloodstone	Libra
2	Taurus	Bull	Earth	Venus	Copper	Sapphire	Scorpio
3	Gemini	Twins	Air	Mercury	Mercury	Tiger's Eye	Sagittarius
4	Cancer	Crab	Water	Moon	Silver	Pearl	Capricorn
5	Leo	Lion	Fire	Sun	Gold	Ruby	Aquarius
6	Virgo	Maiden	Earth	Mercury	Mercury	Sardonyx	Pisces
7	Libra	Scales	Air	Venus	Copper	Sapphire	Aries
8	Scorpio	Scorpion	Water	Pluto	Plutonium	Jasper	Taurus
9	Sagittarius	Archer	Fire	Jupiter	Tin	Topaz	Gemini
10	Capricorn	Goat	Earth	Saturn	Lead	Black Onyx	Cancer
11	Aquarius	Waterbearer	Air	Uranus	Uranium	Amethyst	Leo
12	Pisces	Fishes	Water	Neptune	Tin	Moonstone	Virgo

Foulsham books can be found in all good bookshops or direct from **www.foulsham.com**